DR. ATIYA K. JONES

CHANGE OF VALOR

FEARLESSLY RECLAIMING MY ME!

Change of Valor
Fearlessly Reclaiming My ME!

Atiya's Light Publishing
412 North Main Street, Suite 100
Buffalo, Wyoming 82834
www.atiyaslight.com
info@atiyaslight.com

Library of Congress Control Number: 2019905459
ISBN: 978-0-9968672-5-2

To my Higher Self, thank you for your constant guidance, support, and awakening wisdom. I AM Grateful! I bow and take my hat off to you.

Acknowledgments

I acknowledge the greater that is within me and I honor the divine in others as a reflection of the divine in myself. I acknowledge the oneness of Love and the Oneness of the prophetic community of Love. I acknowledge that all great things are born out of the Spirit of Love.

Still I Rise

*(an excerpt from Hidden Pearls
written by Dr. Atiya K. Jones)*

Shall I walk away
from the game of life,
never to taste
its victory?

Shall I be hopeless
in the plight of all that looks like me
or too ashamed to keep my head up
and my dark, piercing eyes focused
to overcome that which all too often
seems insurmountable?

Shall I gain the courage to walk
even in the appearance of defeat
knowing that there are those who will
tread their paths after me?
How dare I hold my head down
in shame.

For no matter what the game,
there is a light that shines forth
from within me that says,
victory or defeat, still I am.

Table of Contents

Preface

The Awakening and Healing Retreat held in Worthing, West Sussex ENGLAND was a creative child that I gave birth to in March 2019. It was conceived out of a yearning to unfold my vision of a Spiritual and Healing Retreat Center and a call from Spirit. After several conversations and the sharing of my vision, I decided to move toward doing destination retreats until such time we could secure the necessary land to build the center.

This was the first event of this magnitude that I have organized in years. It was the first formal retreat that I had ever hosted. I had small healing gatherings; but nothing like this. Through its planning and participation, much was revealed to me. Words are truly inadequate to express how taking on just this one assignment from the Universe, helped to change my life exponentially. I received very positive feedback from those who participated and took in the whole soul evolution experience. I received not so positive feedback from those who for whatever reason was not able to take in the whole experience.

Each person who participated at any level has their own story to tell in terms of what the experience was like for them. As I spoke with others, perused the many photos and conversations on social media about the "soul evolution experience," something very simple yet profound came to mind after reading something online. People may participate in an event, see the wonderful outcome of something, or witness someone receiving a major award or recognition. They may even tell you what they got from it at the moment of it happening. However, when a person accomplishes something in their life, people see the end result; but they don't see what happened to lead up to that moment. Others are usually not aware of the challenges, the failures, the battles, the sweat, blood, and tears during the process and the fallouts after the event. They don't really get to see what you went through to reach a certain outcome. People rarely have the opportunity to hear the story behind the story.

The Awakening and Healing Retreat for me lived out the true meaning of its name in my life. I said from the very beginning that this was not an event that would change your day or your week; it would change your life, and that dear hearts I can stand on without a shadow of doubt. Personally, I had a profound awakening experience that paved the way for me to begin a whole new journey of healing in my life that allows me to now continue forging ahead in an extraordinary way with courage and an even more beautiful expression of love for self and others.

The week after the retreat, I received a call from one of the participants. She asked me if it was normal to be crying the way she had been crying. I told her yes because it is a release, which is necessary. We did a lot of soul work, some consciously and some unconsciously. She shared with me that after returning home from England's destination retreat, it was not business as usual; she had to stop and deal with some things in her life and consequently took some time out to do so. For me the same was true. I stayed in bed for a week and did not make myself available for any work or to speak with anyone outside of those who the Universe saw fit to offer soul support. During the retreat, I had awakened to some things in my life. Old wounds and emotions surfaced which I was forced to confront and heal. Afterwards, I needed time to process and address my stuff. I was very clear about what my retreat roommate was going through in terms of needing to now release. I was doing the same. Those old wounds and hidden issues surfaced so that they could be healed and any residue left over released. It was a true soul evolution experience.

As I started to do my own process of writing to heal to address the remnants of grief from losing my mother in 2005, what also surfaced was that I was resentful of my father, and angry at my husband. In one of the sessions with a practitioner, she asked me "What are you angry about?" At that time I didn't equate the deep pain in my back between my shoulder blades and the pain in my stomach with anger or resentment. Somewhere along the way as I was in the process of writing my feelings, I ran across a message online that said, it is important after an event or an accomplishment of something major, to share some of the things you faced along the way that helped you to get to the point of where you are now. The message was just a general message somewhere online but it spoke to me in a very profound way. People often see the end result; but when you tell your story, when you tell that part that people are not necessarily privy to, you help them to truly appreciate what you went through to accomplish your goal and also help them to see value in something that they may have taken very lightly or deemed it as insignificant. It was that message from the Universe that inspired me to write, Change of Valor: Fearlessly Reclaiming My ME!

Initially when I started to write, I intended it to be a few thousand words eBook. Yet, as I continued to flesh out what I wanted to say, I realized that there was more I needed to express than originally thought. As I embarked upon the process of sharing my journey with respect to the retreat, I was taken to various times in my life. I noticed a pattern. The very writing of this book was one of the many hurdles that I needed to confront in terms of reclaiming my authentic truth. I like to allow people to save face, but in helping them to save face, I had often done so at my own expense. Therefore, in writing this book, I was confronted with the decision of what approach to take in terms of sharing and how much should I open up publically in this regard. This book is not designed to be mean spirited or a misuse of power. It is soulfully designed to transmute the mess and the test into a profound message for others and a personal testimony of how I dealt with a reoccurring pattern in my life that was blocking my success and keeping me from express-ing my authentic truth.

The Awakening and Healing Retreat which took place in Worthing brought to the surface many emotions I did not realize were bottled up inside of me. From the planning to the event itself, there were many situations and emotions that I was forced to confront and rise above if I was going to succeed at pulling the event off. I learned many lessons along the way. I learned a lot about myself and I learned a lot about others, as well as the community in which I lived. They say that Worthing is a place where people go to discover their self-worth. I have to say, and I do so with a smile, I received one of the greatest lessons in my life regarding self-worth here in Worthing, and for that, I will remember Worthing, West Sussex, the little quaint town by the sea with its hidden treasures that lie beneath the dross and be eternally grateful for my experience there. Worthing is the "destination" where I reclaimed myself.

Change of Valor: Fearlessly Reclaiming My ME! is my story and a behind the scenes so to speak about what I went through in planning and hosting the Awakening and Healing Retreat that almost caused me to give up. I talk about the challenges, the hardships and heartaches, the let-downs, the disappointments, the fear, and all the things I had to over-come in order to achieve my goal. I talk about the various people around me and what I learned about their character. I talk about Worthing, West Sussex establishments and how they receive people from different backgrounds. I talk about my own personal challenges, identity issues, and the biggest mistakes I made in planning the retreat and in previous life situations up to that point. I discuss some of the major decisions I made after the retreat and more importantly, I share life lessons and the beautiful rewards that came after not giving up.

Chapter 1

An Awakening Moment

"It is not the external world that inspires a person or changes their perspective; it is finally awakening to the power and greatness within that moves you to re-arrange your world."

"Oh! I know who you are and I know what you do! The problem is, you need strong ladder holders!" That statement resonated in my soul for days after Stacee said it to me. The more I thought about it, the more I knew that she was right. I was forced to take off the rose-colored glasses and look at my situation and relationships from another perspective. What came into focus as I courageously peeled the pretty, rosy lenses away from my eyes was a pattern of behavior that had gone on for a very long time. I knew that it was time to make some changes in my life, and I had already started making some of them; but I was still unclear about some things and I did not quite know how to put my finger on it.

About six months prior to the retreat, I had already started a very intentional soul journey and therefore I was open to the necessary changes that would put me in complete alignment with my soul mission and my soul's truth. I've never really been afraid of change; it was the unknown that would usually get my britches in a bunch. I needed some sense of stability and security, yet I have always looked to others to provide that for me. When it comes to change, I'm usually pretty open about it. With that being said, I was already very focused on making any changes that were necessary for me to make that would remove what was considered blocks. I was ready to make those shifts that would greatly contribute to my success. And success for me at that moment was to achieve balance in every aspect of my life. I wanted to get out of the funk that I was subtly feeling. Working hard but somehow feeling like I was constantly going in circles or spinning my wheels like a gerbil, trying hard not to get my tail caught between the rungs. No matter how dedicated I was to my craft, it seemed I kept ending up at the same place each time. Although I was ready and willing to make those changes, I just didn't know how or what was really expected of me from the Universe. So, I surrendered. I cried "uncle," waving my imaginary white flag and finally surrendered completely to the Universal flow of things. No matter how weird that might seem for others, it was my normal and the place where I felt the most secure and stable. Now all I had to do was be able to sustain and balance that type of flow, which is easier said than done. Yet, I was up for the challenge and it was and is a challenge indeed! My greatest feat was to learn how to balance between the two realities: Spiritual and material. I was finally much more pliable to the Universal messages coming and not allowing fear to drive me to panic leading to me putting on the breaks. This time I was ready!

"The problem is you need strong ladder holders!" Darn, that was like a brick hurled and hitting me upside my head. Her words cut deep! There was a sting from them that no matter how much I tried to deny, it was still felt. I didn't know at the time if what she said was meant to be a low blow or friendly encouragement. Either way, I grabbed hold of the statement and flipped it every which way I could. It didn't matter what the underlying tone of the words were, they were real and I respected the realness of them. That statement produced internally a profound need and urgency to re-assess my life and my relationships.

The vibration of her words was a deep, penetrating, re-verberating sound that proved to spark one of the most powerful awakening moments for me at the Awakening and Healing Retreat. I pondered over those words for days, and in my deliberation, my mindset slowly started to change because I started seeing things from another perspective.

"The problem is you need strong ladder holders!" Those words in a funny sort of way revived an aspect of my being. They spoke to the sad part—that neglected part of myself that I quite didn't know what to do with. They challenged me to explore the issues around self that had impacted my relationships with others for years. They encouraged me to examine things a little more closely, as well as challenged me to confront issues that needed addressing no matter how difficult or uncomfortable it might be.

Stacee is a big personality. Her workshop and talk was off-the-chain. When it was lights, camera, action, she showed up and showed out! I respect her "boardroom" business acumen and she has a big pair of cojones (kahoonas - balls) as they say. However, no matter how much I respected her professional delivery, I was disappointed not in her performance on the stage, but behind the scenes. As a champion "ball" player, it is not only about how well you can dribble the ball or perform during the game, it is also about your attitude off the court and during practice. While she showed up for the game and played like a boss, she didn't show up during the time when there were no spectators.

As a master trainer and teacher, I assert that, that is one of the most important times to show up because it demonstrates a certain character, attitude, and heart of what real champions are made of. How are you when no one is watching? That is the real test of character. I felt she not only let me down, but also the rest of the core team who was from America down as well. Those were my feelings and I owned them and I needed to express to her not only as a "friend," but as a colleague.

I struggled with bringing up the issue with Stacee mainly because I wanted to avoid any confrontation. We had a disagreement years prior and like most things so I thought, time heals wounds. I sensed some old unresolved energy and I honestly wasn't sure how well things would go over when I expressed my feelings. It was the unknown that had me in a pickle. However, for me to be real and authentic, and as the organizer and host of the retreat, I knew I needed to address it no matter how difficult it might be. Part of me kept trying to rationalize not having the conversation and I was also second guessing myself and my feelings. I ran how I was feeling by a couple of people to ensure that it was not just me being up in my feelings and I sought counsel in what would be the best way of handling the matter without offending and to avoid a fall-out.

Interestingly, before I was even able to approach the two people to run it by them, one of them approached me first. They expressed disappointment in the behavior and loss of respect. They felt that in England it shows a gross lack of manners to not show up to a welcome event when someone is welcoming and honoring you and it equally shows disregard to be late to a meet and greet when you are the guest of honor. And what's worse, he said is that and in order to get you to show up someone had to go and pull you from your hotel room and when you did arrive you showed up looking disheveled. The person went on to tell me that it is not only a slight on me; but it does not help others to respect or take me seriously when my own guests of honor couldn't bother to even show up on time. Ouch! That was harsh; but true. My sentiments were basically the same. Yet, I was trying to be much more loving and gentle about it. He was disgusted.

I ran it by the other person I had in mind. The majority of her questions were more for me and why I was struggling with having the conversation that definitely needed to be had in the first place. She provided safe space for me to clearly express my feelings and she made no judgements one way or the other. She simply allowed me to open up and by doing so I was able to work through not only my own feelings about it, but also formulate a loving and firm approach. In addition, I was able to resolve something that I had not realized was unresolved. She asked me, "Why do you feel you need validation or approval from her?"

I didn't need approval or validation; but that question allowed me to see my own behavior that was perpetuating a situation that has been going on for years not just in the case with Stacee, but with others as well. I was afraid to speak my truth mainly because I did not want to be considered a "bad" person. I wanted to be liked, and in wanting to be liked, I wasn't dealing with inappropriate behaviors from others that impacted me. Consequently, I was helping to create the very atmosphere I did not want to create—disrespect.

When I finally spoke with Stacee, as suspected, she did not take it very well. However, what I am grateful for is staying true to my authentic self and stepping up to the plate to become a better me. I was able to resolve some unfinished business so that I could move on in my life and fully align with my soul mission. I was able to transmute some lingering negative energy and I could not have done that without that situation. It just so happened to take the retreat to pull it out.

That neglected part of me was brought fully to the surface to heal. It took an uncomfortable circumstance to bring it about. As a result, I'm not looking at relational issues idealistically or seeing them how I want them to be. I'm looking at them exactly as they are. This does not mean, I won't give people the benefit of the doubt, it just means that I will make it a point to not escape reality where relationships are concerned or deny what I'm feeling; and that refers to personal or business relationships.

Regardless of the situation with Stacee, her words, "The problem is you need strong ladder holders," were powerfully awakening and while I may not know the motivations behind them, it does not matter because the Universe saw to it that everything that happened was meant only for my greatest good, and that is what I choose to embrace. I AM Grateful!

My Message to You about
An Awakening Moment

It was not the external world that inspired me to change my perspective. It was finally accepting the power and greatness within myself and unapologetically embracing that power that actually moved me to re-arrange my world. When I realized that some people that were around me was not necessarily my friend or even meant me well, I had to make a decision. I decided to stop denying myself for the sake of others. Some of those decisions were very tough to make. So, as I share what was an awakening moment for me, in essence what I'm saying to you is that sometimes it can be easy to sell yourself short or neglect yourself in your generosity or love for others. Many instances you may not even realize that you are doing it.

You do not have to constantly deny yourself, your feelings, or your own sense of comfort to make others comfortable. For some people, that might be necessary in terms of soul alignment, yet for me, that's not my story.

You may have a desire for things to be a certain way or even fantasize about how you feel they should be; but the only way to really deal with issues in your life is to be honest with yourself and others. That is one of the greatest gifts you can give.

Sometimes when you are on your path to greatness and making changes with self, people from your past might re-surface. Often, it is not always for the reasons you might think. Sometimes people you knew way back when or in the past might appear in your life because you have some unfinished business where that person is concerned; and in order to move forward the Universe is providing you an opportunity by bringing them back, to deal with that unfinished business.

Associations, acquaintances, friends, or others may say some powerful words and truths to you. The words can serve as an amazing catalyst for growth. Their motivation for saying what they say or even doing what they do may be one thing, but the Universe can take what may not have necessarily been meant for good and use it to one of your greatest advantages. When you have an open heart and mind and one surrendered to living life according and in alignment with your higher self, the Universe will take the words and actions of others no matter what they are and fuel them to catapult you to the next level in your growth and development.

It is always a good idea to know what you stand for and what you expect. It is equally important to be clear on precisely what others in your sphere expect of you as well. Those discussions need to be had no matter how difficult. It is not a matter of you living up to someone else's expectations of you; but rather to have an indication of how they are perceiving things where you and they are concerned. The only way to get clarity is to be very specific in your language to them and be sure you say exactly what you mean and mean what you say. That way there can be a clear understanding. Do not leave anything to assumption. As the saying goes, "to assume is to make an ass out of you and me."

So, basically what I'm saying is this: Learn to let some things roll off of you like water on a duck's back. There are always going to be people who are not happy with you no matter what you do. There are going to be people who have an opinion of you that is far from the truth of who you are and if you know who you are and the character of person you are, there is no need to give notice or energy to those things that are not a part of your character. There will be times when you are disappointed in others. Check to see if your reasons for being disappointed are based on sound principles and not just your ego getting in the way. Temperament and character are keys in addressing any area of conflict.

At the end of the day, blessings can come from anywhere, even thru people who don't particularly like you. The fact of the matter is ALL blessings come from Source. Therefore, stay sober-minded and be courageous to take off the rose-colored glasses and see things for what they are. Remember that the Universe is in control and the activation of your next level of greatness could be simply a word away.

Chapter 2

Moving in Mid-Air

"No matter the weight of negative vibrations, you can soar above it all and before you know it you learn how to F.L.Y. (First Love Yourself)."

For the past two months or so prior to the Awakening and Healing Retreat, I had been working tirelessly day and night with the planning and mustering up the support needed to make it happen. It was unreal that I could not find one person who would help me do the work. I was not getting the support from home, I was not getting help from the person who volunteered to take on the role of personal assistant, and I was not getting the support from the agencies in the community where I lived. I was feeling that no one believed in me, and sadly no one even cared. There were no responses to emails, telephone calls, or invitations to sit down and talk about what I was doing. You should have seen me. Some days I was sitting in my living room with my lips poked out like woe is me. The scene from the movie, *The Color Purple*, sums it up about right.

"I can't move. I can't move. I need to see her eyes. I feel like once I see her eyes, then my feets can let go of the spot they stuck in."

My higher self must have looked down on my lower self and in the voice of Shug Avery said, "You sho is ugly!"

Of course that was my ego whispering and I was harboring feelings of being beat down. I tapped into the various agencies within the community who promoted support for the types of events I was organizing. On paper and in the public, our focus seemed to align. Yet, every last one of them I reached out to ignored me.

"Universe are you for real?" I asked.

"Yes, now keep going!"

After conducting hours of research trying to connect with at least one agency in the community who would be willing to partner with me, I ran across Discover Worthing. I sent them a flyer and to my delight, they agreed to post it on their site. I engaged in communications with a young lady at Discover Worthing who agreed to meet. After a few emails back and forth, the communication on her part abruptly stopped when I attempted to pin point a day and time for a meeting. I decided to make another appeal, and took a walk through town to personally go to the office. This time I had the pleasure of meeting Judy, who had recently joined the local authority as the Councils' Visitor Experience and Marketing Officer. She is promoted as helping to bring the marketing in line with Worthing's changing demographics and boasted as bringing a fresh approach to tourism in the area.

Out of the many agencies in the community, Discover Worthing is the only one that sat down with me. After our meeting, which was very positive by the way, Judy referred me to the Community and Wellbeing Team. She said what I was doing was precisely what they look to get involved with and said that she would help to make the connection between me and the team and assured they are able to support this type of event, although she is not sure of the level of support that they would be able to provide. At that time I was looking for them to get involved in at least one of five ways: 1). Become a community partner (£2,500 commitment); 2). Promote the event in their circles (FREE); 3). Secure a table at the Wholistic Wellness Fair (£180 commitment); 4). Attend the Wholistic Wellness Fair (time commitment); 5). Take out an ad in the program booklet (between £50-£1,000 commitment). I was even willing to give a table to them as a way to help expand my reach in the community.

During our meeting, Judy said that what I was doing is definitely within the scope and remit of the Communities and Wellbeing Team, and that it would be great to sit down

with them as we are aligned. I excitedly awaited the opportunity to meet with the team.

I attended the Worthing Chamber of Commerce Business Show and my husband directed me to a table that the
Adur-Worthing Council had set up. I had an amazing
conversation with Angela, the Economy & Skills Officer. We
spoke for about twenty minutes and it was a very positive
dialogue. As I shared the focal points of the event, she re-
uttered what Judy said to me. "You are hitting every target
that the Communities and Wellbeing Team focuses on. It
will be great for you to sit down and speak with them."
Angela appeared to be very excited about what I was doing
and even invited me to get involved in another program that
she was organizing. She admitted to me that the council has
a challenge when it comes to diversity and getting the multi-
cultural community involved. I mentioned to her that I
would be honored to help and as such diversity and being
able to pull diverse teams together is one of my strengths.
One of my areas of expertise is community development and
team design.

The two conversations sounded very promising. I believed the conversations with both Judy and Angela was the
start of a mutually beneficial relationship. Things were
starting to go in a very positive direction and I was really
happy about that. However, what I thought was a positive
turn was actually followed by the run-around and buck being
passed from person-to-person, a bunch of lip service until

eventually they just ignored me altogether. After the two seemingly very productive and progressive conversations, you can imagine how surprised I was to be snubbed. There was no doubt in my mind that I was being snubbed either; and no matter how much I tried to keep a positive face and outlook, the truth is I was hurt and ticked off at the same time mainly because I was once again smelling the stench of this sickening disease that keeps rearing its ugly head.

Angela never followed through with making the formal introduction she promised to make, nor did she copy me on any emails sent as she said she would. The day we spoke she so happened to provide me with the name of a young woman named Mel, who was the Neighborhood Manager on the Communities Team. So I reached out to her when I did not hear back from Angela. Mel emailed me back and again sent me to a different person. "I think it would be useful for you to link up with our Wellbeing /Public Health lead Janice Hoiles so I have cc'd her in to make contact with you."

First it was Judy, then it was Angela, and now it was Mel. I still hadn't had the chance to sit down with the Communities and Wellbeing Team in person or even receive an invitation to sit down. So when I received Mel's email, I asked her should I wait to hear from Janice or should I reach out to her? Mel indicated either way would be fine. I said that I would wait to hear from her that day. In the meantime I heard back from Angela indicating she had been off work for the past week, but that she hopes something comes of it.

I also heard from Janice, who was the Families and Wellbeing Lead at the council.

"Your event sounds interesting; do you have more details you could email please? e.g. where it's being held, who you are targeting, what the overall aims are, etc."

I was very pleased to email Janice the details of the event again. As I had emailed them to everyone I spoke with up to that point at the council. So, not only did I direct Janice to my website where I had been diligent to disclose all information and details on the site, I also attached flyers and all written correspondence. Also in the context of the email, I answered her questions as well. It was apparent by then that no one wanted to "deal with me" or definitively commit to supporting the event. This is what I wrote to her:

1. The event is being held at the Chatsworth Hotel in Worthing between March 19-23.

2. During this time there are four cooperative events going on within the context of the one larger event. They are:

- 5 day, 4 night Awakening & Healing Retreat (March 19-23, 2019) - targets women from various parts of Europe, U.S., and Canada.

- Women's Empowerment Day (March 20, 2019) - targets women from Worthing and surrounding areas.

- Retreat-4-the-day (March 21, 2019) - targets men and women from Worthing, surrounding areas, London and other communities in the U.K. as well as closer European countries (e.g. Ireland, France, Germany).

- The Worthing Wholistic Wellness Fair (March 21, 2019) - targets men, women, and families from Worthing surrounding areas, London and other communities in the U.K. as well as closer European countries (e.g. Ireland, France, Germany).

THE OVERALL AIM AND PURPOSE OF THE EVENT(S) ARE AS FOLLOWS:

1. Hold safe and loving space for women to not only identify, heal, and release deep seated emotional wounds often leading to psychosomatic illnesses, but also to explore issues around self and how it plays out with others; to share the secrets to awakening their voice and reclaiming their abundance; to get to know a whole new version of themselves; and to

embody the essence of their Soul Mission and true self.

2. Improve the health and well-being of individuals and their families through access to information, awareness campaigns, and prevention strategies.

3. Engage in community development/Tourism efforts and actively demonstrate such through meaningful participation, collaboration, and the implementation of strategies for those within the community, in various other counties in England, and abroad.

4. Create supportive networks for immigrants, who live, work, and/or have businesses in Sussex and build bridges to help with integration into the community, as well as facilitate a pathway for those born in England and the perspective counties to value "the inherent worth, dignity, diversity, and abilities of all individuals, families, groups and communities in their area."

5. Collaborate & Establish Global Partnerships through programs such as Destination Abroad – Global Educational & Professional Exchange Program, a 360-degree educational and professional empowerment program which provides an opportunity and interna-

tional experience for students, professionals, and individuals in the community at-large who excel in their schools and/or communities; have an entrepreneurial spirit and leadership qualities, show a commitment to higher ideas, and who evidence dedication in the demonstration of their accomplishments and community service.

The response I received via email from Janice was, "Hi, many thanks for the additional information, which I have shared with colleagues. Kind regards." Again, there was no commitment to sit down and have a conversation, although I had requested a meeting to sit down on numerous occasions and discuss the event and how we could collaborate. Not one person on the Communities and Wellbeing Team expressed a willingness to sit down and talk. Because Janice's email was not clear on what the next step would be, I asked.

"So will you be contacting me back or will someone else from the council contact me?"

Janice words back to me were, "Hi, it looks an interesting event however it doesn't quite fit with the services I'm responsible for, so I've shared it across the team. If there is someone else who wants to link up with you they will be in touch. Good luck with the event! Kind regards."

Janice's words did not set well with me and perhaps I was missing something. So I sent another email to Janice, however at that point, it was clear to me that they were just passing the buck and they were unwilling to meet face-to-face and discuss this event or any other one for that matter. This is my response:

> *Hi Janice, thanks for getting back to me. Will you please outline precisely the events that the Communities & Wellbeing Team focuses on? When speaking with both Judy and Angela these events fall within the remit of the Communities and Wellbeing Team and actually hits the targets of what that particular team focuses on. However, thus far, I have been sent to several different people and the impression I'm starting to get is a passing the buck and no one at the council interested in supporting the event which is of great benefit to the community. These events deal with wholistic health and wellbeing, community development, diversity, women empowerment, immigrant supportive systems and integration into community, tourism, and education. So I'm sure you can appreciate I'm a little puzzled. Perhaps I have been referred to the inappropriate departments. Please advise what the Communities and Wellbeing Team's function is and what is actually in that area of responsibility. Thank you.*

I did not receive an immediate reply from Janice. However, at that point Judy of Discover Worthing stepped up to say they were willing to help out with the areas that fall under their remit. Judy agreed to attend the meet & greet and help to welcome the international delegates to Worthing. In her email she attempted to deflect from the pointed questions I asked Janice. Not to mention I found it to be distasteful to have this conversation via email when it could have been simple for the team to agree to a meeting to sit down and discuss and reach some sort of understanding. In her email, Judy wrote:

As I am sure you can appreciate there are a vast number of wellbeing / wellness events which take place in the town and staff only have limited time to support with promotion. I don't think it's a matter of passing the buck more that your event is independent from the council and as such may not fit directly with current projects. I think it's really useful to keep both Discover Worthing and the Community and Wellbeing team in the loop with this and forthcoming projects - tagging us in social media is always an easy way to spread the word and we'll then support as we can.

While I was appreciative of Judy's response, she is not a part of the Communities and Wellbeing Team and because my question was specifically directed to the team lead, it was only fair that the response come from the leader of the team. She did not readily respond. Therefore, in my reply to Judy, I made sure that I included her in the response to Judy's assertion.

Happy Day Judy, thank you for your email. I have noted that you have agreed to come and do the welcome at the meet and greet and I really appreciate and value what you bring . . . I can appreciate time management and events on other projects that you are committed to. However, I would love the opportunity to be able to sit down and discuss the diversity plans and what the council is currently doing to reach diverse backgrounds. What are the responsibilities for outreach and engagement with ethnic minorities and multi-cultural organizations? If you do work with this sector, please provide examples of how you've worked with them and what steps would need to be taken to form collaborations and partnerships to engage professionally and respectfully, rather than turning a blind eye or ignoring the matter? Also, what guidelines are in place for funding each year for engaging multi-cultural projects? What are the targets and responsibilities and what are you doing as a council to encourage more diversity?

Finally, what is it about what I'm doing that's forcing a reaction in a manner in which I feel locked-out, ignored, devalued, and not part of this community and just an immigrant, despite I pay taxes to help employ members of the council to serve our community?

This is of importance and relevance to me for numerous reasons.

As a metaphysician, I pay special attention not to the superficial qualities of beings such as color, ethnicity, nationality, gender, etc., but rather on the very fundamentality of their existence and/or the way they exist. As I interface with beings in a health and wellbeing capacity, I find that many are usually disaffected by similar issues. The common theme is to find some semblance of love, support, acceptance from mainstream society, and to feel a part of the collective whole in the communities in which they live. However, the reality is often seen as quite the contrary and more detrimentally social isolation. Likewise as a metaphysician I provide holistic life counselling and pastoral counselling as well as other holistic health and wellness modalities. Fundamentally when people feel disenfranchised or deprived of rights and privileges that are otherwise free to others of a borough, city, or country, it invariably impacts their being and how they exist. There is a link between social isolation, racial discrimination and poor mental health.

I have an extensive background in community development and outreach, relationship building and team design, program development and implementation, personal and professional development, and fostering positive discussions bringing out successful outcomes. I have trained and worked with one of the best if not the best diverse psychiatrists in the world, Dr. Carl C Bell, who absolutely knows how to impactfully help to transform the lives of disaffected populations of people, especially those from multicultural backgrounds. I have worked on large-scale, multi-year consulting interventions with tremendous political, economic, and social impact for hundreds of people, and have engaged thousands of people in efforts to make complete life transformation leading to becoming more productive members of society. Furthermore, I have a high level of emotional intelligence and understand the profound impact when people feel locked out.

My focus is to ensure there are platforms and systems in place that people from diverse backgrounds can access to thrive, be productive, and share their expertise and gifts, and feel useful, which ultimately helps to cultivate overall health and wellbeing. To that end, when there are no systems in place or the systems are challenged at best, my focus is to collaborate and partner with the necessary entities, agencies, and organizations to ensure these systems are put in place for the benefit of the collective whole and then to implement programs and strategies that engage people in areas of their talents and passion for the betterment of the whole.

While I stand on the principle of charity begins at home and then spreads abroad, I actively seek to first develop in the community in which I live, as well as support the businesses in the community in which I live, and I encourage those I interact with to do the same. Next, I build bridges and systems of support across communities to enhance and enrich experiences and to build and strengthen relationships. My goal is to see all people regardless of culture, ethnicity, gender, nationality, etc. to thrive and be included in the collective whole rather than be excluded whether it is by design or a result of cultural incompetence and ignorance. We as a community are no greater than the least of us; therefore I make it my business to help heal social injustice and actively become a part of solutions to help all members of a community thrive.

It is important to note, however, that while I stand on the principle of Worthing, West Sussex first (because this is where I live and work), my work is global, my network is global, and my conversation is global. I don't know about you, but I like to talk about the positives of a community, rather than highlight its weaknesses. I like to discuss ideas and ways to strengthen certain areas and then follow that discussion up with solid action. My mother use to say quite frequently and challenge leadership to "put your money where your mouth is." God rest her soul. As a person who spent over 35 years in the university system and an award winning poet, she was very eloquent and dynamic in demonstrating there are many ways to "an end." And the more ways you learn the richer and more spectacular the adventure!

Until and unless there is value "the inherent worth, dignity, diversity, and abilities of all individuals, families, groups and communities in the area, will there truly be community. I appreciate your time and attention and look forward to having progressive dialogue with the council and communities and wellbeing team about the above outlined.

Janice finally replied. However, her response revealed the same profiling that often exists in the absence of diversity at a given table. Furthermore, she avoided answering the questions I presented.

Hi Dr Atiya, the Communities & Wellbeing Team is a large team which aims to reduce inequalities within our communities through specific work streams. The wellbeing services we run, as one of the areas within the Communities & Wellbeing Team, are funded by Public Health West Sussex to deliver specific evidence based activities to reduce health inequalities by actively targeting people who are the least likely to use services. We receive a lot of requests to support events and only do so if we: need to promote our services, the event is specifically targeted to reach one or more of our groups and we have the available resources to do so. I have copied the Manager of the Communities & Wellbeing Team, Jacqui Cooke, into this response, in case she would like to follow up with you regarding the wider remit of the team which includes: Crime & Anti-Social behavior, support of the Voluntary & Community Sector, community engagement (around issues such as long term unemployed; digital skills, prevention of homelessness) and social prescribing. With kind re-gards.

I was still trying to give the Adur-Worthing Council and the Communities and Wellbeing Team the benefit of the doubt. However, it was their unwillingness to even have the decency to sit down and dialogue that showed me they were not interested in engaging the multicultural community. I felt that they were simply trying to tick boxes on their reports and project accountability for monies received to do a job, but in actuality not doing the job they are funded to do. So here I stand a Black woman and immigrant who approached the Communities and Wellbeing Team to sit down and dialogue and then when they demonstrated the unwillingness to even sit down for a brief meeting or a face-to-face, I called them out. Finally, as a tax payer, I asked for accounta-bility. At this point, it was no longer about the Awakening and Healing Retreat so much as it was about access and representation. My response to Janice at that point, before I was to decide if I wanted to take the conversation to another level was this:

> *Hi Janice, thank you for your response. I don't believe you responded specifically to my request for information or request to meet with the Communities & Wellbeing Team. Also, may I quote you on your email?*

Once again, the buck was passed. In Janice's next response, she referred me to yet another person on the Communities and Wellbeing Team.

> *Hi Dr. Atiya, I'm unsure what additional information you are requesting - I outlined the main areas of the Communities & Wellbeing Team in my previous email. The best person to speak to regarding the team, or about meeting with the whole team, is the manager of the team, Jacqui Cooke, as I previously emailed - I have cc'd Jacqui again to this email. Jacqui will be able to pick up & respond to your queries when she is back from leave tomorrow. Kind regards*

When I first approach the council with an invitation to sit down and speak, it was the first week in February 2019. Here it was now February 28th and still not one person even willing to sit down and provide the opportunity for me to get "access" to information and support. Jacqui came back to me, but it wasn't until a week later. On March 8th, this is the email message I received from Jacqui, the Interim Head of the Communities and Wellbeing Team.

> *Dear Dr. Jones, I have been passed the emails that have gone back and forth between yourself and Janice and would like to suggest that we meet up so that we can outline the role of the Communities and Wellbeing Team and also understand your work and how these might compliment [sic] each other. Jo, could you please find an hour for Janice and I [sic] to meet with Dr. Jones please. Thanks.*

I was very grateful and was feeling like, "Finally, someone with some sense." I thanked Jacqui and let her know my availability for early the next week. However, when Jo came back to me, she advanced a date of April 1st which would be a week after the event. I just had to laugh to keep from crying. I could not believe the blatant disregard or stupidity? I wasn't quite sure which it was. One thing for sure, I was sensing racism. I sent a message back to Jacqui asking her, "Now you do realize that this date is after the event?" Once I sent that question via email that was the point where the communication process completely broke down. From where I was sitting, they were not interested in an honest dialogue and the lack of response to my last email demonstrated to continue pushing, on that level anyway, was an utter and complete waste of time as far as I was concerned. I decided to let them stay in their little bubble and let someone else come and deal with that. I was determined to do the retreat regardless. So, my bigger question—the one that I had wondered about since moving to Worthing was answered in my brief interaction with the council and the Communities and Wellbeing Team.

"Why are there so many homeless people on the streets in Worthing?"

Here you have a town with an estimated total population of about 114,212 people. The last census report reveals that in 2011 when there were about 102,562 people, of those

6,558 of those people were multicultural. I'm sure that number has risen since then. Yet, when you look at the representation on boards, at events, decision-makers, in lead offices, the existence of people from multicultural backgrounds are not visible. You don't see any! There is not an accurate representation in Worthing. So here I come along, not only multicultural but an immigrant and I have the audacity to put on a wellness event and pull people together from various backgrounds. Who do I think I am? I'm "independent of the council" which is the words written in one of the emails from the council and they in their own words stated that they receive a lot of requests to support events and they only support them if they have the "need" to promote their services. Where does the citizen's need fall into that equation?

Angela stated that the challenge of the council is engaging the multicultural community. That's incorrect! To be very blunt about it that's a lie! The problem is, there is an unwillingness to engage that population of people. So now I can understand why one young lady I met named Monique who works as a care worker, was livid and I ended up spending an hour listening to her rant about how with all the services in Worthing, she was not able to access the necessary support for her elderly mother who happened to be a Black woman. All they wanted to do, according to Monique, was "dope" her mother up instead of addressing the real issue of her health condition.

I made one last call for support to finally have a sit down with the supposedly well-connected head of the Worthing Chamber of Commerce after a long chase and track down, wrong email addresses, and non-working telephone numbers that he provided me with. He said he would check into his network to see what they could do, but I never heard from him after that meeting. No follow-up email, no phone call . . . nothing. Interestingly, I was walking toward the train station about a week after the retreat and he did not recognize me but I recognized him and called his name out. He was very startled and scurried away from me. I'm sure he figured it out later. Anyway, during out meeting, he said that Worthing is a very conservative community and not as innovative as those from America. He said what the English tend to do is stand by and watch first and see how you do on the first event before they support you, and then what they will tend to do is support the next one. That to me was just a sloppy excuse and a load of bull crap.

There are agencies put in place and funded to do a spe-cific job. They will either stand on what they say they do regardless of your racial makeup or nationality. The group of speakers and presenters pulled together for the retreat was a very diverse group of people. I demonstrated the ability to galvanize people from various walks of life. Yet, no matter how well things were organized, how professional I was, and how effective I was at communicating the message, it felt like a complete lockout. If you want to know the truth, it was a complete Blackout. At every event I attended, up to the point of the retreat to rally support and attendance, there was no one that looked like me. Not only was there no one that looked like me, there appeared to not be any immigrants as well. The rooms were pretty much filled with English folk. I also learned that even in their networking groups, they have a practice of lockout, where they do not allow more than one type of the same business. So if you have a business similar to what is already in their networking group, they lock you out and close the door to you.

How dare I think I was going to come to town and not only change the face of the various rooms, but how dare I think that I was going to bring new and innovative ideas and creative ways to pull various people together for the greater good. I was naïve to think the status quo even wanted a multi-cultural presence. So when the head of the Worthing Chamber of Commerce said that the players in the community will stand by on the side-lines first to see how you perform, before they help in any way, that did not set well with me, especially when it was clear that they were not performing well at reaching the professed hard-to-reach areas of the community. What was classified as the hard-to-reach was not hard to reach at all. I was able to reach them quite easily and connect with a diverse group of people with very little effort. My naivety was in thinking that they wanted to truly reach the multi-cultural community. To "stand by and watch first," was a tactic of lock-out in my opinion.

My philosophy is this, if you don't bother to suit up and show up for practice, you don't get to play in the game. I even wrote the royals of Sussex. Although I was hopeful, I really didn't expect a timely response from them. I lost faith in Worthing. I gave them the benefit of the doubt; but through the tactics that were employed to what I feel was a lock-out; it is hard to think that little misunderstandings are actually just that.

Even though the community was not interested in supporting the events, I was set on supporting the community. That is just what you do when you get involved community development. There were several businesses closing up shop in Worthing. I did not want that for "my" community. So when the Universe placed the retreat in my lap, other ideas flooded my being as well and the ideals were raining generously. I was eager to share the wealth. However, I do feel Farrah Gray when he says; he will only support those who support him. I was set on using local suppliers for everything possible during the planning of the retreat. That was my mantra even against the face of opposition. I just feel like charity begins at home and then spreads abroad. Therefore, I was adamant about supporting businesses in the community. All I wanted was some support in some way no matter how small, even if it was to just attend the Wholistic Wellness Fair for free. The host hotel was supportive. Yet, I realized that while the host hotel is the most beautiful hotel in the community, it is not the "chosen" hotel of the status quo. I sensed some snickering around that as well. I'm not sure why or the history. However, when I would discuss where the event was being held, the response I often received was something like, "Oh aren't we posh." And if the words didn't roll off the tongue, it was the look that spoke a thousand words in the silence. I found it to be rather interesting.

There were many fundraising activities going on to help support the retreat. One fundraiser was the Pay-it-Forward Movement, which helped to generate some really great and positive energy. This movement created much community attention, so much so, that another group in the community, not associated with the Awakening and Healing Retreat, popped up afterwards advancing a Pay-it-Forward Movement. This raised some questions. In an effort to learn more about this new group, I found that I was locked out of that group and none of the organizers returned calls or messages. Also after the Awakening and Healing Retreat, the group interestingly dissolved.

Anyway, part of the Awakening and Healing Retreat was to be live streamed. This happened on day three of the five days. People from all over the world were presented with relevant and valuable information, as well as practical take-a-ways to apply to their everyday life. I hired a company from the Worthing community to produce the program magazine. During the negotiations for the cost of the printing and the final agreements, Gemini requested me to have payment upon delivery. So on the day before the event was to start, I had cash in hand of £300 to pay the cost for printing. When I received the call that the delivery person had arrived, I came with money in hand ready to pay as requested. When I asked the total amount owed for the work, the representative from Gemini told me that I owed nothing, it was all taken care of.

"Wow!" I said.

"Have a great day." He responded.

A big wuss, I cried all the way back to the restaurant where I was having lunch with Lakichay, one of the delegates who arrived from America two days early to assist with whatever I needed help with. It was one of those ugly cries but one for a good cause. With joy and relief and a sense of breakthrough I cried because in my mind I was still fretting over how I was going to pull everything off. So Gemini helping in that way was a blessing. I shared with Lakichay that I was not charged for the printing and was told it was taken care of. At first I thought perhaps Tony from the Chamber of Commerce might have had something to do with it. My husband asked me the same thing, so I know my thinking wasn't far-fetched at all. I was very touched and naturally assumed that either Tony or Gemini was paying-it-forward. As I was sharing with Lakichay about what had just happened, we agreed not to try to figure it out, just receive the gift and keep it moving. This was the power of the Pay-it-Forward Movement. I was thrilled!

I was not back at the restaurant ten minutes when I received a follow-up call to see if I received the books. The representative from Gemini said they just called to make sure I received the magazines. I told them yes and was very thankful for their generosity and they assured me I was very welcomed. I told them that I would send a formal thank you letter after the retreat.

I was very happy at that point. As part of the fundraising, I had been advancing the movement of "Pay-it-Forward" and as a result I was able to generate a lot of positive energy and several people were inspired to pay-it-forward. In Worthing, the Chatsworth Hotel paid forward a room for the "Meet & Greet," as well as the use of the projector and screen for the event. Between Gemini and the Chatsworth, it was very encouraging, especially after getting the run-around from the council.

Three days later at the live streamed event, I acknowledged the support from the Worthing community and also named people and companies on the international broadcast. However, the day after the live stream, I received an invoice in my email from Gemini Printing for the program magazines. The invoice was for £230. Now, any other time I would have questioned things more thoroughly. Yet, because of the Pay-it-Forward Movement, and being told I did not owe anything for the printing and that it was all taken care of, and then also receiving a follow-up call as well ensuring I received them and when thanking them for their generosity, being told it was no problem, I naturally thought Gemini was paying it forward.

I can't say that I felt stupid or embarrassed. In truth, I felt used and somewhat played. I honestly thought that the magazines were paid forward, and the telephone call that followed appeared to me to be a confirmation of them being paid forward. I showed up with the cash and did not have any expectations of me not having to pay for the magazine. I was told they were taken care of, I believed just that. Therefore, believing that the magazines were in fact paid forward, I gave copies away to attendees at both the Wholistic Wellness Fair and the Speakers Showcase, instead of using them as an income stream as I initially intended.

When I received the invoice, I was dismayed. Of course, I responded to it and opened dialogue about being told I owed nothing and that I even received a call right after delivery to see if I received them. I shared how I went through the whole process of thanking them for their generosity and support and telling the guy who called from Gemini that I would send a formal thank you letter afterwards. The gentleman who rang me from the company told me I was welcomed. So after I sent the email in response to the invoice, this was the response concerning such.

Regards the invoice and payment — I am sorry for any confusion. Our drivers are not allowed to take the payment — what we usually do is call ahead and arrange to take payment by card over the phone.

Trudy is very sorry that she didn't make contact on that point to en-
sure all was clear. It would have been wonderful if we could have
adopted the pay it forward mantra but sadly we are not in a position
to do that at this time as the business is committed to a number of
other charitable causes.

I felt even more deceived and misled. I was told to have the funds available upon delivery when I arranged for the job to be done. I agreed and followed through with that agreement. Yet, upon delivery, when I tried to pay them, I was told that I did not owe anything. Yet, four days later, which was after the live stream, I received an invoice in my email. Mind you, this was four days later from the date of delivery. It was public knowledge that I was advancing a Pay-it-Forward Movement. Heck, as I said earlier, there was even another group who started a meet-up advancing their own Pay-it-Forward Movement in Worthing. This group had nothing to do with me or my event, but it popped up shortly after I started the movement in the area to generate some positive and loving energy in the atmosphere. If the delivery drivers are not able to take payment, then why tell me to pay the driver upon delivery? What I think happened in someone decided to pay it forward and then someone else didn't agree, and then there was an internal disagreement.

Let's just say, I ended up feeling like the jackass with this magazine situation. Not only did I announce to people they were paid forward; I also gave them away as a result of thinking they were paid forward. Now the really feeling like the ass part, is in the fact that the invoice now has to be paid from my own pocket. I don't think it was just a matter of confusion. Honestly as I just mentioned, I think it may have been some internal disagreement.

The majority of the support for the Awakening and Healing Retreat came from outside of Worthing. To be more specific, people travelled from London to attend; while Worthing did not even pass through. While I appreciate Judy, I did not feel that the community was supportive. The leadership did not support it and likewise the citizens did not support it. One young lady named Millie helped to round up some people support. The financial support, all except for about £500 of the $7,000 was raised from America. The majority went toward paying the hotel and the rest on the participants. Money was raised in dollars; yet bills were paid in pounds, so as you could work out, there was a gap. It took more dollars to cover bills that were in pounds.

Throughout the process, I was mainly seeking support from the Worthing community to attend the event and/or to either take out an ad or secure a table. It was hard not to take it personal. It felt like there was a concerted effort not to support the event. I even got an email from the chiroprac-tor's wife who along with her husband was the very first people I sat down with to invite their participation, and ultimately they fobbed the event off. When the event started getting a lot of traction in the public, she emailed me and said, "Oh what I must have thought about them." Given the calls and emails I received that day, I know she was just trying to see if I was in a good space with them. I felt she wanted to see if "we were good." I was warm and kind. She mentioned in the email that they would come and support. However, there was no sight of them that day at all. The same was true with others businesses in the community. I sensed a nice-nasty from many. There was a whisper that supposedly came from one of the people who was manning a table at the Wellness Fair. She was working the table for a local company that I gifted it to. Her sentiments were, "What a waste of time." People come with their own expectations and often when they do not experience what they expected to experience, they rarely see the overall blessing of a situation. Her table made sales that day, as I was one of the people who purchased from her along with others. The Wellness Fair was meant to accomplish much more than monetary gain and it most certainly achieved what it set out to do. For that I AM Grateful! I imagine if money was the only thing on a person's mind, she may have been disappointed. Yet, the blessing is the table was provided "in-kind."

When it finally got down to the wire, and I realized that the hotel was taken care of, I just wanted to ensure that people who I gifted booths to would have a constant flow of people coming through to support their products. After all, the majority of them came from London, which is about two hours away. Every table in the room had sales that day, some more than others. However, I was very grateful and happy for them. The majority of the feedback was favorable.

The participants of the five-day Awakening and Healing Retreat were provided three spa/healing treatments. I turned one of the hotel rooms into a beautiful treatment room and hired those who had booths to do the treatments. So the participants received an EMS workout, reflexology, and a body massage. I initially was going to do Reiki on the participants, but I had given so much energy away, that I just could not muster up the energy to do the sessions, so I replaced Reiki with the body massages. Since I only mentioned spa treatments in the planning, it worked out fine. It just added to the budget, which caused me not to be able to immediately monetarily pay one of the speakers until a couple of weeks after the event. After all was said and done, with the added pounds to the budget, and the mix-up with Gemini, we ended up in the red by £330. Although, I did not get paid monetarily at all for the work, my payment came in so many other ways and I AM Grateful. However, this too shall change. I've planted good seeds into the Universe and I trust that all is well.

My Message to You about
Moving in Mid-Air

I had to accept the fact that no matter the weight of negative vibrations, me soaring above it all—the racism, jealousy and envy, those who for whatever reason wanted to place stumbling blocks in my way, or people who didn't want me to succeed for whatever reason, I had to first love myself. That is what flying is all about. I had to remain steadfast and do what I was inspired to do!

What I'm saying here is this. When the Universe gives you an assignment, you have to just kick on with it even if there is no one else visibly around backing you. If the Universe gives it to you, then you better believe that a way is also made for you to succeed. By all means knock on all the doors that you are inspired to knock on; but if none are opened to you then keep moving, keep working. Rest assured, there is a better door that is for you. As Tyler Perry once said, "Thank God for closed doors because that means that it was not for you." He further said that if the wrong door is opened to you, you will never reach your destiny.

You have a door to your destiny, and that is the only door that is necessary to have opened. People become disappointed when they have expectations of others. When the Universe gives you an assignment, don't expect others to understand or get on board. It's your assignment and no matter how many people you want to bring along with you, it may not be for those you want to bring with you. The Universe will bring you the right kind of help and surround you with the right kind of people who will help to propel you further to your goal. Some of those people may not come with a peachy disposition. Sometimes they may be a pain in your backside, but that might be the necessary thorn you need to accomplish your said goals.

Don't get frustrated at the obstacles. Look at them as opportunities to grow. Know that you are equipped to overcome everything placed in your way. Let your focus be on aligning with the will of the Universe and achieving what you set out to do. Remember that you are a winner already, and no matter how bleak things may appear to be on the surface, all you have to do is keep walking in your authority and your victory, and soon others will see what they could not see at the beginning.

Chapter 3

Pushing Past Fear, Doubt, & Disappointment

"You have to decide if you will yield to the gravity of your lower self or turn toward the power of your higher self to help you navigate the waves of life."

T o say I worked extremely hard during the planning process is an understatement. Although I hid it well, I started to doubt if I could pull this whole event off. I did not question my capability or skill level to bring it about; I questioned whether I would continue to have the tenacity and strength to make it happen without the necessary support system. After a while, I wondered if it was all worth it. There were so many times I wanted to give up. I just could not see a way through. However, no matter how hard it was, something inside me pushed me to keep going. Believe me when I say it did not get any easier. It got harder and harder and the closer to the event it got, the higher the stakes became. Yet still there was something inside me pushing me to not be confused by what my physical eyes saw and to trust the Universe and the process.

The one thing I was sure of was that after a certain point, whether the event happened or not, the hotel where the retreat was being held was going to charge me anyway. So there came a point of no return.

Early on in the process, a former client, asked me to let her help. It was one thing to believe in my healing abilities and spend an hour a week with me, but it was yet another to go on a serious journey with me that required a bigger time and energy commitment. Anyone who has ever worked with me in any capacity can attest to the life-transformational experience. They can also verify that it is very hard work and requires one to be ready to confront their own personal issues. I have even been called a slave-driver in the past. Yet, to be fair, I'm not that, and I do not give anyone else something to do that I myself would not do or has not done. Manifestation takes hard work and I honestly don't believe people realize that until they work to manifest. I might make it seem easy, but believe you me, it is not easy! You have to want it more than the hard work it takes to make it come alive. I have a lot of swat equity in everything that I have ever manifested. People do not necessarily realize that so, this is one reason it's important to value your products and end results. Some people can start something with you with very good intentions, but they sometimes lack the stamina or the faith required to endure through all the changes and challenges.

I learned very quickly that the self-proclaimed PA wasn't ready for the ride. She bailed like hay. It just so happened she ditched me before she even got started good. As a client, I charged her on a sliding scale. A session that I would normally charge about $150 per hour for, I charged her only £30 per hour. For several weeks she was a faithful client. After a while, she stopped coming because she could no longer afford to pay for the sessions. Some time passed by and then one day she called me up and wanted to go to lunch. She volunteered to pick me up and she took me to this fabulous café on the sea front. It was her treat. During lunch, I did a lot of listening, similarly to what I do in sessions. However, this time it was over lunch.

As I listened, somewhere in the conversation she offered to help me. She said she needed something to do, something more meaningful. She also shared with me that her son has been asking to come to see me. He liked the changes he was seeing in his mother, so he wanted to visit Dr. Atiya as well. I cannot begin to tell you how that touched my heart. I should not have been surprised because of the quality of my work; but the truth is, I was surprised.

I made an appointment to see her son and did not charge her for it. We started to meet about the event. It did not take long to see that she did not see the vision. It was evident throughout her presence in the planning process. I had to constantly motivate her and continuously defend the price points of the event. It was exhausting. It was frustrating because not only was I confronted with her not being able to understand the vision or see the value, my husband took a hands-off approach throughout the entire planning process until the final hour. He showed up for meetings, but did not engage and demonstrated a very poor disposition throughout. His ego got the best of him in my observation and it was like dealing with a spoiled child throwing temper tantrums because he couldn't be in charge. With her lack of faith, a language barrier, and just not being able to keep up, eventually, I just had to accept the fact that the two of them were not ready and therefore, I allowed the meetings to take a hiatus. In the bigger scheme of things the meetings were great social time-outs and went very well if we treated them as such. However, from a work standpoint, they were not productive at all and nothing really ever came out of them except a nice break from the work.

Yet when it was time to work, there was not really any follow through from either of them and eventually I made the decision to not take the weekly three to five hour social breaks at her house. There was too much to get done and I had to take charge of my time and manage my workload so that I could assure the event happened. In hindsight, I really do not believe either of them truly understood the vision, nor could they see the possibilities. They lacked faith in their own abilities and also lacked faith in me. She bailed completely and to this day really has no idea how things turned out. I did speak with her finally, and she stated she struggled to believe in herself. My husband jumped on board at the final hour. He stated that he didn't have faith in his abilities. The thing is, I believed in both of them, and had no doubt of their ability to kick but in what they were charged with doing. I realized that I had more faith in them than they had in themselves. Yet, no matter how much you believe in someone and see their potential, they must believe it for themselves. This situation really drove that point home. In truth, even if they didn't believe in themselves, all they had to do was follow my guidance and they would have discovered some amazing things about themselves in the process. They had the tools, yet they did not know that for themselves. No matter what I said or did, it didn't matter at that point. They just were not ready.

The two people I thought were on my side, honestly wasn't there when it really mattered the most. They allowed their insecurities in themselves to defeat them at that moment. To be completely honest with my feelings, I was very disappointed in how my husband handled the matter overall. Although I keep telling myself that it is not how you start but how you finish. In truth I don't fully believe that. I appreciate what he was able to deliver in the final hour. Yet, if he had just believed more in himself, we could have surpassed the goals in that situation. Also, it would not have been so darn hard. Even if he did not believe in himself, if he had just trusted me more and believed in me, he would have not only discovered his own hidden potential and abilities, but he would have been able to experience the power of two people working together for a common goal.

It is not fair for me to deny or suppress how I feel about the situation. Any time you set out to accomplish something of consequence, it's usually not easy. Ease or difficulty is a matter of perspective. The question is, will you or won't you. The difficulty factor comes in when you fight against your own will to achieve. When a person decides to accomplish something, they don't put focus on how hard it will be. The focus on what has to be done to get from point A or point B and then go to work doing their best and letting the Universe do the rest. As I see it and from my vantage point, what matters the most to me in that process is having someone who is willing to stay the course no matter what things look like on the surface. What matters to me is to have someone there who trusts me, trusts my vision, and willing to stay the course from beginning to end of the project and not letting anyone compromise the intent or the integrity, and not allowing anything or anyone take you off course. That is true loyalty. I am loyal and I want loyal in my corner. Once the Universe says to be, all we ever have to do is just be. The truth is we have that same power. We can manifest anything we desire when it is in universal alignment.

Working with me requires a commitment and a solid sense of self or a willingness to develop a solid sense of self.

If you say you are going to show up, then dammit show up and give it your best. If we fail, at least we gave it all we had. If we succeed, then it is a win for all of us. When we win, I compensate others very well. This I know. When we fail, I have usually carried the load of failure. However, I don't fail! I always win! I say that because even a failure is a win in my book. Through failure are life transformational lessons. Success and failure are relative terms and depending on how they are viewed in the mind of those working with you, will depend on whether or not they give their all. If a person proceeds as if success is inevitable they will not succumb to fear, doubt, or disappointment. I've learned that success and failure are states of mind. Anything in life you work toward, you must have the right state of mind.

It is important to see the vision of the one who walks out front. However, if you don't see it, you must trust the person out front to guide you to victory. Otherwise, you either get in the way causing a nuisance or you bail. I experienced both of these situations in the process of planning the Awakening and Healing Retreat. I rather a person be honest and tell me straight up no chaser, "I do not believe in your vision." That way, I can excuse you at the beginning. If you say you believe in the vision, mean it and move like it! If you somehow lose sight of the vision, let me know and I can help you re-awaken to it. After all, that is one of the things I do!

I rather be disappointed in things like the coconut milk carton being put back in the refrigerator with one swallow left, or sitting down on the toilet and then realize that the toilet paper on the ring has only one square left. Now that kind of disappointment is only a **S**ugar **H**oney **I**ce **T**ea moment. To be disappointed in people you believe in and care about is another matter altogether.

I could not allow disappointment to hold me back. I was not going to let myself down and that is what had to matter the most in that moment. Others might give up on me or even themselves; but there was no way I was going to give up on myself.

My Message to You about
Pushing Past Fear, Doubt, & Disappointment

In the process, I had to make the decision as to whether I would yield to my lower-self or turn to my higher-self. There was no backing out one way or the other; I had to make a choice. Fear, doubt, and disappointment are lower-self vibrations and since I chose not to yield to it, that meant I needed to confront the negative self-chatter in order to navigate the waves that were rolling on in my life in this instance. I was resolved in turning the fear into faith, the doubt into determination, and disappointment into fulfillment.

The point here is to not allow fear and doubt to cause you to turn away from your objective. Yes, things can get pretty tough, and sometimes you can feel like you are all alone; but remember that you are never alone. The same God that brought you to it can also bring you through it; but you have to be willing to persevere. Your will to succeed has to be stronger than your doubt. "Let your faith be stronger than your fear." Let your determination be stronger than your doubt; and let the vision that you have been given be a torch lighting the way in dark moments.

Should others who you thought were with you bail, don't bat an eye just keep pushing on. Keep pushing until you reach the finish line. As it has been said, "The race is neither to the swift nor the strong, but to those who can endure until the end."

To endure is to persist and remain steadfast, even in the face of difficulty. If you are the one holding the vision, then it should not matter who does not "get it," or understand, if you can see it, then it is up to you to be it!

Chapter 4

Choosing a Supportive Community

*"If birds of a feather flock together, then perhaps you might
want to assess who is in your flock!"*

I think I finally understand the meaning of not casting
pearls before swine. I've made the mistake over and
over again, but I think this time, it finally landed. The
community of Worthing, West Sussex helped me to grasp
that lesson very well. There are many agencies and services
in Worthing that are geared toward the health and wellbeing
of the community. Likewise there are agencies that are
focused on tourism, women's issues, and family programs.
No matter the plethora of agencies in the community that
boast of their support of such activities, it was not demonstrated when the opportunity arose to get involved in some
way no matter how large or small with the Awakening and
Healing Retreat.

There is a saying, if someone tells you who they are the first time, believe them. When I first moved to Worthing, I experienced blatant racism. I just did not want to believe that it could be like the Republic of Ireland, so I dealt with the matter and moved on, not wanting to taint my excitement about moving to this little quaint town by the sea. When I first arrived in Worthing, I was taken to a radio station with the idea to meet with them about broadcasting my show on there as well as advertising. Prior to any acquaintance or any sort of introduction being made, I was told at first sight that I will never be on that radio station. The woman who so freely made the assertion, didn't even so much as know my name or who I was, she looked at me and made the determination. My husband and I had been walking, so we were in workout gear. Yet, our professionalism was still evident in our presentation and our manner of speaking. It was very apparent in her words that she profiled and stereotyped us. We were appalled. However, we decided to handle that situation without giving it too much energy and continued our journey in Worthing. However, we should have taken a little closer look. Not that it would have changed our minds about living in the community, we would have moved slightly differently. After living in the Republic of Ireland for three years, we just did not want to believe that we would have to deal with that type of drama in England. Ireland was a wake-up call and there was no way I was willing to deal with that type of treatment in England.

Another clue in terms of the attitude in Worthing came when my family came to visit and my auntie and sister were walking in the town center, and were referred to as 'rubbish." People can be so ignorant sometimes. My auntie is a retired professional from AT&T, and my sister has her Master's Degree in Education Administration. They were deemed "rubbish" because of the color of their skin. It just really goes to show the stupidity of some people. The silly thing is that according to some studies, England has the lowest literacy rate of first world countries. The silly thing is that the people referring to them as rubbish probably did not even know how to spell the word.

Racism is not only ugly, but it highlights the ignorance of the people who are trapped into such narrow and limited thinking. I continued to refuse to acknowledge that there is a very real issue in the town. Honestly I felt it, but I chose not to give it any energy.

Seeing with my own eyes the diversity in the community and doing my research on all the wonderful things that Worthing has to offer, I insisted on holding the Awakening and Healing Retreat in the community in which I lived. Charity begins at home and then spreads abroad, right? Yes, this is what I kept telling myself to consistently feel the need to defend my position every time Ingram stated, "I don't know why you insist on holding this event in Worthing." It was necessary for me to give Worthing the benefit of the doubt. I prefer tried and true and if I haven't tried the person or place, I don't know if it is true or not. There is a Biblical principle outlined in 1John 4:1 that says, "*Beloved, believe not every spirit, but try the spirits whether they are of God: because many false prophets are gone out into the world*" (King James Version).

From a metaphysical standpoint, what this means to me is that it is important to try a person's word to see if it is true and whether or not they stand on what they say. There are many people who talk a good game, but when it comes time to deliver or prove what they say, they come up short.

Worthing, West Sussex came up short! Those in the community who said they would support the event did not. The agencies who advertised that they participate in such activities did not stand by what they said they support. I realize that all situations is not necessarily a result of racism. However, in this case I do honestly believe that with the community agencies it was more about diversity than anything else. In other words, an event being hosted in the community by a Black woman from America is not some-thing that they feel their dollars or in this case pounds or time is worth contributing to, especially when the beneficiar-ies or participants are mainly those from diverse back-grounds. We did not fit the criteria from a racial and nationality standpoint. So when the echo came about the event being a waste of time, it didn't surprise me because the room was diverse and the most diverse I had seen at any event in Worthing in my year of living there. I intentionally went about ensuring that there was representation from a wide sector of the community. I achieved that goal! The whisper supposedly came from an English woman, not to mention that she was in fact in the room and was not excluded like so many others who were present in the room are at other events. I did not lock out anyone! Consequently, what showed up was a diverse group of people.

Discover Worthing showed up like they said they would. Kudos to Judy for making her word bond and making a personal appearance at the meet and greet to welcome guests from America. She allowed Worthing to save part of its face. All but one of the speakers showed up. I was happy to see many of them shared the event on their social media pages and in their circles. I would have liked to see the local speakers push their individual workshops more though. The reason being is that my focus was on helping them to expand their sphere and shine their light even brighter and to demonstrate how they can create additional revenue and money streams using their gifts and talents.

I'm willing to stand on the front line with you, yet you must be willing to stand on the front line of your own life. One participant from England commented about how those from America had more light. She said that we have a certain type of creativity where we are not stuck in a box when it comes to manifestation and we have more energy and excitement about what we do. In planning the event, I noticed that some people living in England are plagued with a suspicious mindset and tend to think people are trying to get one over on them or use them. One person I gave an ad to actually initially declined because he said he did not want to be "obligated." His thinking was when someone shows you kindness you are then obligated to them. I took him to task on his faulty perception and shared with him that thought process is most definitely not my mindset or way of thinking. When I give, I give from my heart not expecting anything in return from that person. I know that what I give will be returned tenfold. It doesn't matter who is the source of the giving that comes back, because all things come from Source.

I also learned that some people won't do anything or will hesitate to get involved if they are not getting paid money. Yet, there are so many ways to "get paid." It saddens me when people make money the number one focal point and deny the very thing that they are praying for because they are unable to see past "money" to discern a blessing that could in fact be the answer to their prayers and offer the rewards and blessings far greater than they ever imagined. As a result, they mishandle situations and people because of spiritual blindness.

Serhan, a 20-year old Brighton University student from Turkey, was a classic example of pushing his individual workshop. He brought his entire family with him as well as a media crew who interviewed him about the event. It was very shameful that the media outlet gave him a sorry excuse not to run his story because there were not at least 40-50 people in the room when they took the photograph. I think that was just hogwash and another slap in the face. I sensed his frustration and disappointment, rightfully so. I stopped by the restaurant and asked Serhan to be sure to share the article with me once it was published. That is when he told me that the media outlet decided not to run the story. He was visibly disappointed. He has since closed the restaurant and to my understanding now focusing on school, while his parents are moving back to Turkey as his mother will be serving as Mayor of the town in Turkey where they will be moving.

I spent the majority of my time raising revenue to ensure the retreat happened and chasing speakers for information. I did not know how to get the word out in England. The one person I knew who could get the word out wasn't on board in the early stages to do so. He was focused on his own stuff (his words) and since he said that I did not check with him prior to deciding to do the event, he did not feel he needed to. I know without a shadow of a doubt that those words came from ego. So it is not even necessary for me to put energy into that statement. I just continued the work we said we would do and allowed Spirit to guide the process.

I gave several speakers the opportunity on many occasions to make a small contribution or pay-it-forward and at a minimum requested that they invite their friends and family to attend their individual workshop. The bottom line is I did not have the support I needed.

During the planning stages of the retreat, I did my best in spite of the lack of support to maintain a positive outlook. I was scared of failing. I was worried about looking bad and having my word fail. What was even more frightening was the thought that no one would show up and I would be left standing with over a £3,000 hotel bill. Even more horrifying a thought was to have the one person who believed in me and demonstrated it by purchasing her airline ticket immediately to attend the event before any plans had commenced, show up, and it was just the two of us. Trust me when I say, I had a contingency plan if that would have been the case.

I was not about to let that happen, I kept working and trusting the process. Knowing that Lakichay believed in me and had already purchased her plane ticket was enough to keep me focused and trusting in the Universal plan. I kept the vision in the forefront of my mind and I kept envisioning her here in England in the forefront of my mind. I was "scurred" (in a St. Louis accent); but I trusted the process. I recall asking one of the brothers that I was speaking to, "What if I don't raise all the money needed to pull it off?" He said, "So what if you don't? What is the worst that can happen? You learn for the next time." When he put it that way, it did not seem as big a deal.

However, it was a big deal because I did not want to be a disappointment. And that is an issue that I had to work on—

not wanting to disappoint people. Ironically, the more I focused on not being a disappointment to people, the more I disappointed them.

With all the activities I had going on in the community and the planning of the retreat, no matter how I felt, Spirit kept nudging me to keep going, and not to be frazzled by what my physical eyes were showing me. My Higher Self was nudging me to keep going and to have confidence in my ability to pull it together. Therefore, no matter what echoes I heard, I kept going. I kept working. As a result, idea after idea continued to flow. Eventually the idea of a contest came to mind, and it was the contest that ultimately served as the vehicle that proved to be resourceful in raising the necessary funds to pull off the event. The contest provided an avenue for others to attend the five-day event as well. I AM Grateful. There were several events happening simultaneously with each one contributing to the overall success.

I gave just about everything away. The sisters from America rocked and came through like champs. The hotel donated a room and showed generosity in other areas. My husband raised a few hundred pounds on his end, which turned out to be very timely during the five days. I'm appreciative for that.

By the time the retreat arrived, I was already exhausted from the amount of energy it took to pull it off up to that point. However, when I reflected on the overall situation, I went back to the words, "You need strong ladder holders."

After all was said and done, I had to assess the situation from a non-emotional standpoint while addressing some very real emotions that I was experiencing . . . anger, frustration, disappointment, sadness, feelings of unworthiness, lack of value, and the list goes on. Yes, that was my ego, and no matter how I was feeling, my ego was not going to put me in a prison of negative thinking.

I asked myself the question, "Who is holding my ladder?" When I looked at the hard truth of the matter, I realized that I really did not have any ladder holders. Sure, I had people around me who supported the best they could, but in truth, I did not have what I needed in my life to reach the heights of my own potential. No matter what talents I have, how creative I am, what value I bring to the table, I could not be effective without having strong ladder holders, or so it had been said. So, I looked around my sphere and ask myself the question, "Who is holding my ladder?" You know what I realized? Not one person was holding my ladder; and that opened the way to learning one of the biggest lessons of my life.

My Message to You about
Choosing a Supportive Community

I had to examine who I was flocking with. It was important for me to assess the sort of company I was keeping.

While I was not keeping company with any one person or people in particular, I discovered that there were many people in my sphere that was not serving me well.

While to be in relation with others is a fundamental human need, who you relate to and with is very important. You are who you are, and that does not mean you do not work on being a better you, but if the people you consistently relate to does not see the inherent value in you, then it is necessary to examine that. People who do not value or respect you will not support you. Sure they may give an outward appearance of being behind you; but do they really, deep down support you?

It is important to surround yourself with people who believe in you and who will encourage you as well as share with you areas in which you can improve to reach your goals and objectives. That support cannot always be silent support either; it must also be demonstrated in tangible ways. Having a supportive community of people in your corner generates a very positive energy that even when you do experience self-doubt or concerns of whether or not you can accomplish something, you will have people in your corner that you can have honest dialogue with and will not be pessimistic or judgmental.

It can be very lonely to go after your dreams and not have anyone there you can bounce things off of or at least vent to, especially in times of uncertainty. When you need to vent, and there are times you might need to do that, you do not want to do so with people who will encourage you to give up. You want good listening ears for venting; you want great counsel for when you need to problem solve, you need great companionship when you want to celebrate small victories; you need great friends when you need encouragement.

So make pointed and wise choices of people you allow to get close to you. Building relationships that are mutually supportive and satisfactory goes a long way in life and being fulfilled. Failure or defeat, a good supportive community will point out the victory in every defeat; and will help you see the wins in every perceived lose.

Chapter 5

A Life-Changing Lesson

"Knowledge is not the acquisition of information; but rather the practical application of principles learned in the process. Wisdom is a far greater gift to possess."

A sking myself that question led me to Dr. Samuel Chand, a leadership consultant and dream releaser. In his book, *Who is Holding Your Ladder*, he talks about how he was waiting to attend a meeting at a church, and during his wait, he gazed out the window and noticed a man standing on a ladder painting. As he watched the painter, he saw that the man was only able to paint a limited amount of space. As he looked down to see who was holding the ladder, Dr. Chand said that although he could not see the person or persons holding the ladder that probably went down eight floors or more to street level, there must be someone holding the ladder. This got him to thinking as he watched the man painting the exterior wall of the building reaching to only the height of his arms over his head. The painter was already standing on the extension part of the ladder; but he could tell that the painter was able to climb higher still but was uncomfortable. In order for the painter to finish the job, he would need to muster up the courage to climb higher. However, another point that needed to be considered was although he could climb higher if he wanted to, his ability to climb higher was also impacted by the ability of the ones down below being able to hold the ladder securely and firmly. In order for him to be secured on the ladder, the ladder had to be held securely. In addition, the painter had to be able to trust that the ones holding the ladder could do so without question (Chand, 2015).

I ran across Dr. Chand's book in my quest to answer the question about who was holding my ladder. I hadn't read the entirety of his book, nor had I even heard of it. However, as I pondered Stacee's words to me, and as I questioned my own self truthfully, I had to determine for myself what a ladder holder meant for me and what I needed to do to ensure that I had strong ladder holders if in fact I needed some.

First of all, I must take full responsibility for not having ladder holders. I realized in hindsight that I spent years guiding and empowering people while also being a ladder holder for them. Yet, I failed when it came to providing for myself. I was freely giving to others; but I was neglecting myself and denying my own needs and wants in the process.

I was being a hero to others; but a zero to myself. Consequently, I was inadvertently teaching people to use me and not value me. So in essence what was consistently happening was that when I needed support, I wasn't getting it because people just assumed I had everything I needed because I was steady giving. As far as others were concerned, I had what I needed and whenever I posted or invited people to purchase my books, tapes, attend my events, or support my cause in any way, they did not see the value or necessity in supporting it, because at the end of the day, I would eventually give it away anyway. If they wanted anything from me, all they had to do was hold out long enough, and they could get it for free.

It was like I was this great big mammary gland that people could suck from over and over again and it was free. I was dependable and just about anyone could depend on me to provide without very little requirement. "If you get the milk free, why buy the cow?" My mother drew that point home when it came to shacking. Yet, that is a principle that can also be applied to other situations as well.

I had to finally admit to myself that I was handicapping myself and others. I was handicapping them by not requiring of them what would make them better. I was handicapping myself by not valuing myself. In turn I was creating a culture in my sphere of the lack of real and authentic value and creating a mindset of poverty. I was not giving people the chance to value or see the inherent worth in what I have because I was giving it away and not showing them how to value me and my offering. And what made it even worse is that they were starting to resent me for it. I was in essence to some degree leading from behind because I was pushing people up the ladder and even in some cases carrying them up the ladder and then going back down it to hold it for them. Oh how foolish when you think about it. The song goes, God bless the child that's got its own. I have my own; I just had to learn how to really let my own work for me. I have everything I need to succeed, I just had to learn to respect and honor what I have; and part of respecting and honoring what I have is to place a value on it rather than giving it away so freely. I must treat it like it is priceless, because it is. By doing so, people can truly be blessed by the gift that I am and the gifts that I have to offer.

Requiring people to pay for my offerings gives them the chance to invest in themselves. That is one of the greatest benefits I can offer them. It teaches them that they are worth it. I cannot expect for someone to value something that I myself is not valuing. How do I show value in what I do and what I produce? I require fair payment and compensation unapologetically.

It took the planning of the Awakening & Healing Retreat to wake me up to areas of my own self-demise. The five-day retreat allowed my feelings to be heightened so that I could more clearly see where I was making a mistake. I was confronted with the truth that for the majority of my life, I had been holding other people's ladders, while neglecting my own. I was giving my power away and in some cases allowing others to take it. I had to shift that paradigm. I must shift that paradigm!

My Message to You about
A Life-Changing Lesson

Life has taught me that no matter how much information a person has acquired or stored, knowledge does not come into play until one is able to take that information and put it to use or practically apply it to one's life. Yet wisdom is a far more precious commodity and I have to honestly say, I became wiser not only by my own life, circumstances, and experiences; but also by watching and learning from others.

When you take full responsibility for the things in your life, it gives you the opportunity to also present a solution to what you feel is not working. It is natural sometimes to want to put others before you. However, when you get into the habit of always putting others before you and it is done to your own detriment or at your own expense, that can be characterized as foolishness. How can you be effective in helping anyone else or taking care of anyone else if you do not take care of yourself first? Some people will tell you that is selfish or that you are being self-centered, but that is not the case. Wisdom teaches us that self-preservation comes first.

It is important to give from your overflow. I say this because when a person is a giver, they will often give until it hurts and they will deplete themselves. In some situations they may become resentful. Yet that is not the proper spirit of giving. Therefore, when you give from your overflow, you also feed your own soul in the process. One of the greatest lessons with respect to giving is that when you give, it shall be given unto you so in essence to give is to sow seeds for the benefit of your own soul; yet give without depleting yourself.

Chapter 6

Confronting My Truth

"There is only one. All others in your sphere are simply reflections of different aspects of who you are."

D r. Chand makes a lot of sense in the little bit of his book that I read. I appreciate what he says about the ladder and the ladder holder. His words helped me to realize quite a bit, as well as helped me to understand why I did not have any ladder holders and to assess whether or not my path even include ladder holders. In his PowerPoint presentation on ladder holders, he stressed the importance of choosing leaders. He said that doing so would be a very important decision. I can see that. He also asked the pertinent questions, "Is someone holding your ladder," and if so "What kind of person are they?" The questions he asked in the PowerPoint presentation helped me to ask myself the right questions for my own particular situation. So I rephrased and directed the questions to myself (Chand).

- Do I have to remind the people around me or who work with me constantly?

- Are the people who are in my sphere intentional doing what they do or are they haphazard or casual?

- Are the people in my sphere able to stay focused or are they easily distracted with other things?

- Do the people in my sphere actually see or understand my vision?
- What types of people are actually around me and in my sphere? What are their characters like?

- Are strong, attentive, faithful, firm, and loyal leaders what I really want and need?

I thought long and hard on these questions and let the truth be told, there was no other way, I had to change! I didn't like the setup and the setup wouldn't change until I changed! I was ready for change. So I asked myself the questions in that moment and I answered with the truth as I saw it. It was time to look at everyone and everything else, including other aspects of myself. I was not getting away from it. Things had come full circle. Interestingly, that was the number of the room I stayed in during the Awakening and Healing Retreat—360! Since there are no such things as coincidences, it was most definitely a signpost from the Universe to me.

So I opened completely up for an interrogation by my higher self. I was not backing down. I was ready! The honest answer to those questions left me with no other alternative than to change my sphere and do so quickly. I turned the focus on myself and what I needed and desired first.

When I look at what I have been able to accomplish without ladder holders or without the visible support system I felt I so desperately needed, something inside me clicked. It became clearer while writing this book. I really needed to confront self. Why was I holding on to things and people that did not mean me well? Why was I secretly seeking approval from others and in some way needing validation from them? I had to deal with self.

My Message to You about Confronting My Truth

In confronting my truth, I came face-to-face with myself. You can put rose-colored glasses on and pretend all day long; but at the end of the day, if you cannot be honest with yourself, then who can you be honest with? No matter how hard it is to see things the way they really are, you must look at the truth of the matter and stop trying to sweep things under the carpet. It is what it is. Once you accept the reality of how things are, only then can you actually do something about it.

Some people may not like you or what you stand for; but be true to yourself and stand on that regardless of what others might think or feel about it. You need neither approval nor apologies to be who you were born and purposed to be. If there are things about yourself that you do not like or that does not serve you well or help you to be the best you can be, then you change it. Don't change for others, change for yourself and to be a better reflection of the vision you have for yourself.

Chapter 7

Learning to Let Go & Trust

"Letting go of past pain and negative experiences and believing that all will be well may feel like closing your eyes and jumping, but not quite sure where you're gonna land."

Fear is a really very strong obstacle to overcome. Yet, when you go about making a change, not just in your circumstances, but in yourself, you have to face the fear. I have been making myself over for decades; but nothing like the changes required now since the retreat. Things had come full circle. For me, what that meant is learning to love myself and being authentic and true to myself. I did not really have to change me; I had to change how I was handling me. For years, I had allowed accusations of being self-centered and wanting to be the center of attention stop me from stepping out in the forefront as I should. I became content being in the shadows the majority of my adult life mainly because I did not want to be misunderstood or called self-centered. I was unkind to myself and unjust to myself from the fear of living up to the words that haunted much of my life. When these types of words come from those you love and trust, that makes it even harder. Regardless what anyone has to say about it in their lack of security in themselves, I'm not self-centered and I have never sought to be the center of attention. I spent my life trying to disprove the lie and in the process I wronged myself in almost every way possible. I kept holding other people's ladder when my ladder in many cases was the one that should have been held. I did not doubt me; I doubted the worthiness of me in comparison to others. Consequently, I always chose the other people over myself. Sadly in some cases, I did the same with my children when I should not have. Sometimes our greatest lessons in life come from our children. I am grateful for them and that they chose me as their mother. I have amazingly beautiful children and I am very proud of them. They have taught me much.

The Universe inspired the Awakening and Healing Retreat. It is surreal. I had no idea the wealth of information that would come from that space. There has been so many times in my life that I doubted myself; but in planning the retreat presented a new level of anxiety. Like I said earlier, it wasn't that I doubted my ability to organize it, I was confident in that part. I doubted whether I would have the necessary support to follow through with it and I lacked the confidence that people would respond the way I wanted them to. I took risks, a lot of them. I took those risks believing that the support would be there, but secretly I was very afraid it would not be. When I saw that I was not getting the support hoped for, I became disappointed. I started asking myself questions about what the problem was. I could see success in my mind's eye. My vision took me to amazing heights. I could see the other side of the accomplishment of the retreat. I could taste it. I could feel it. I believed in it. I had an eagle's view.

I was not afraid to climb to the top. I was ready for it. The challenge was that I was not able to get there without the necessary support. I needed someone who believed in me and my vision and who was willing to roll up their sleeves and work alongside me. I did everything I could to share the vision with others and to invite them to become a part of something that was greater than us all. That was my thinking, anyway. I could not fathom why no one was willing to support this great cause.

I spent a lot of energy working around the male ego, trying to motivate and inspire others, and creating traction hoping that someone would jump on board. No matter how high I was willing to climb, no matter how clear my vision was to me, or how real of what I could see, taste, touch, smell, hear, and sense, it still was not enough to get the visible support.

I believe it helps tremendously to have people who believe in you and your vision to make it to the top. No matter how many risks you are willing to take, I believed it makes it so much easier when you have a visible support system. When I took a long hard look at my situation, I could not see that visible support system. I have people around me who support me in the way they can as stated before; but the kind of support I'm talking about is the kind where I can climb up the ladder to reach my full potential—the kind of support where my movement can match the speed of the ideas flowing through my mind; the kind where the brevity of my actions can match the strong desire yearning in my soul. As I looked around, I didn't see any ladder holders. So I simply could not stop at the question of, "Who are your ladder holders?" I had to look a little deeper. Having ladder holders could not be the only way.

I finally had to let go of what was familiar and start trusting. I could not solely rely on what my physical eyes could see or my brain could comprehend. I had to let go and trust that there is a reason for why things were playing out the way they were. Instead of trying to control everything, the Universe kept nudging me again and again to just let go and trust. Try flowing with it. That is when I finally was able to accept things as they were and stopped trying to make them what I wanted them to be. I found acceptance. It was at that point I realized that I did not have to work so hard. I simply needed to tune into what I already knew and understood intuitively. I needed to remember that I have everything I need and want within me. My challenge was to use what I have for myself first and not the other way around. That meant to let go of that which no longer served me externally and trust in the internal power—that mighty force and power within me.

My Message to You about
Learning to Let Go & Trust

I learned to jump . . . close my eyes and jump and trust that all will be well. To me that is what letting go of stuff I was holding onto for years was like.

In this journey we call life, there are many instances where we must let go. It is a hard thing to do sometimes. Some people are so used to holding on to crap from their childhood or past relationships that they forget what life can be like without the pain and negativity. Also, they prevent themselves from experiencing the true beauty that life can offer. If you are one of those people who are struggling to let go, I encourage you now to confront whatever issues are within that interferes with your ability to experience the amazing highs that life can give.

Work through the pain and make a firm decision that you will give happiness your energy and deprive negativity. Decide now to walk in your power and your passion and live an incredible life in balance and in harmony with the Universal flow. Sometimes pain in unavoidable, yet don't hold onto it like it is covering your nakedness. Work through it and be free from its residue. Stop making excuses and stop holding on to it like it is a badge of honor. Let it go.

How do you let go of pain? Write down the issue. Write how you feel about it, how it made you feel, how you contributed to the issue, what would make it right, what you need to happen to be okay, how can you make what you need to happen in your own life, and then decide to let it go. Once you have written it all down, now go shred it or near some water burn it and then spread the ashes to be cleansed by the water.

Now, after all is said and done, CHOOSE to forgive, to let it go, to trust, and to be healed and happy. Once you do that, the thing of the past is just that—a thing of the past. It does not need to be resurrected.

Whether you are a man or a woman, learn to let it go. My girl Erykah Badu puts it this way . . .

> *. . . I know sometimes it's hard*
> *And we can't let go*
> *Oh when someone hurts you oh so bad inside*
> *You can't deny it you can't stop crying*
> *So oh, oh, oh*
> *If you start breathin'*

Regardless of what type of negative bag you carrying or holding on to, let it go, let it go, let it go . . . "garbage bag, grocery bag, Gucci bag, paper sack bag, nickel bag, backpack on your back bag, booty bag, cheeba sack bag, plastic bag, baby bag, Ziploc bag, Fendi bag . . . let it go, let it go, let it go!" Stop holding on to stuff that does you no good. If you don't, "One day all them bags gone get in your way" (Erykah Badu).

Chapter 8

The Power of Metaphysical Science

"All that is real may not always be experienced by the physical faculties we call senses. There is a wisdom beyond that which is evident materially."

I'm a metaphysician and one engaged in the practice of Metaphysical Science. Having a doctoral degree in Metaphysical Science, I am well versed in the subject matter and practice. I know first-hand that things don't stop at the physical. Behind every physical and seen reality there is a spiritual and unseen reality. When I stay on my square as they say, it is easier to not lose sight of a power behind what our physical eyes can perceive. In my daily life, I seek to not solely rely on the material of what I can comprehend carnally. It is important to go with what I know and utilize fully the information that I have at my disposal.

As I said, the Universe inspired me to host the Awakening and Healing Retreat. It came out of a yearning in my soul. It wasn't for anyone else to do. It was for me to do. There were people who crossed my path along the way who provided pieces of information or imparted various things needed along the way, but none remained for the most part as mainstays. I am grateful for those people. They came and they left. They passed through my life and when they did, they received a little and they gave a little. I continued on my own journey no matter who came into my life or who left it. In some instances, I slowed down, but I didn't stop. When I let go of external and internal baggage, I sped up again because I became lighter. Paraphrasing what Louis, Jr. said to me, "So what, if you have to slow down sometimes, as long as you keep going, you are still moving, and that is what's important. Just don't stop."

There were more times than not that I could not see my way through. Yet, by completely trusting the Universe I learned to stand firm, not on a ladder being held by a ladder holder, but by learning to trust and keep climbing even in the absence of both the physical ladder and the ladder holders. If you want to know what it's like to walk on water, try putting on an event with a zero budget and no support system. You can get a glimpse of what it was like for Peter, when he walked on water for the first time. However, the minute he took his focus off of the Master, he started to sink down into the water. The reason Peter started to sink was because he did not have the faith within himself that he could actually walk on water in the first place. When he was shown how to walk on water, he trusted so much in the Master that he stepped out there and walked on the water. The Master did not hold Peter up in the water. Peter did that himself. He did it because of his faith in the Master. Imagine if he had that kind of faith in himself.

Peter didn't move on his own accord. He took action only at the urging of the Master, and he did not move according to his own faith but moved according to his faith and trust in the Master. Peter relied on the power of the Master's faith to hold him up. The Master was Peter's ladder holder. Peter was not able to move beyond what his Master encouraged him to do. He did not realize that he could do that and more of what the Master could do.

Without the ladder holder, Peter could not continue to walk on the water. What Peter and so many others fail to understand is that living faith is about having "assent of the mind to the truth of a statement for which there is incomplete evidence." Assent usually comes after consent. Consent is the ACT of the will. Assent is the UNDERSTANDING and AGREEMENT of the will. In other words, parents or legal guardians give consent for a minor child to participate in an activity. However, "Assent is the agreement of someone not able to give legal consent to participate in the activity." The child assents to what the parents must legally consent to. In the case of Peter and the Master, the Master consented to Peter walking on water first because Peter did not have the requirement necessary to walk on water on his own accord. He had faith, but it was not in himself, it was in the Master. So the Master was the custodian or guardian of Peter's faith and was in essence working to help Peter develop faith not in the Master, but in a higher power. And thus there is a biblical text that says, "...greater is he that is in you, that he that is in the world" (1 John 4:4, KJV).

The Master consented to the activity and Peter assented . . . He agreed. Once Peter turned away from the Master, he started to sink in the water. He relied on the ladder holder to hold him up. There was something missing inside Peter which required him to look outside of self for permission to do what he in actuality already had power within himself to do. Yet, being a child in faith, still learning to walk in the power of faith, he relied on the power of the Master in that instance.

Active faith was necessary for Peter to continue to walk on water without the Master. If Peter was to develop active faith, he would have realized that he did not need a ladder or a ladder holder. He could have become the Master.

Now faith is faith in motion. Now faith is when the mind can see what the physical eyes cannot see. Yet, if you only believe in what your physical eyes can see and you focus all of your attention on what you can only see with your physical eyes, you are like Peter serving an outside master never learning the lesson of self-mastery. Likewise, if you only believe in the unseen or the vision in your mind's eye and have yet to be able to manifest that unseen or your vision to the seen reality or materially, you are equally handicapped. Having the wherewithal to manifest is a clear demonstration of your faith in action.

In the song from the Prince of Egypt sung by Mariah Carey and Whitney Houston, *When You Believe*, there is a line that says, "We were moving mountains long before we knew we could" (Schwartz and Zimmer).

"Now faith is the substance of things hoped for, the evidence of things not seen" (*Holy Bible Illustrated*, Heb. 11.1). "Now Faith," as described in this biblical verse is a form of telekinesis or psychokinesis—the ability to move things with the mind.

Learning to stay in motion and continue to climb without the comfort, support, and stability of a physical ladder or ladder holder, requires you to become the Master. Metaphysical Science delves into the very nature of what exists, how it exists, mind versus matter, substance versus attribution, and possibility versus actuality. It deals with classical quantum physics and genesis. Quantum physics is about matter and energy at the sub-atomic scale or the level of that which is less than an atom. Genesis is the very origin or beginning of how something is formed.

People create unintentionally so they are usually not aware of their power. Others would rather take part in something that already exists and shy away from the creative process. It takes a lot of energy to create. We conceive things all the time, but to manifest it takes a whole lot of energy and sometimes it takes more energy than a person might be willing to give. Yet for me, I stay in the creative zone. I'm just learning now how to simplify the process and simplifying the process is about lightening the load and getting rid of what weighs me down or drains my energy. It means to keep a clear space for creating and manifesting.

The retreat started as an idea, a thought, a concept, a vision, a Universal assignment. I had a zero budget, which basically means I had nothing but the idea to start with. Every step required me to trust the process even though there was nothing solid to rely on. There was no beginning budget. At every turn, it required the ability to see what needed to be manifested in my mind's eye and then go to work to put energy towards its manifestation. I never knew how it would unfold, I just had to keep believing that it would unfold and work as if success was inevitable. I had to become the creator, the master, and have faith in a Master plan.

Ninety-nine point nine percent of the people looking at the situation from the side lines (Facebook, Twitter, LinkedIn, Instagram, and other social media outlets) were not even aware of what was happening before their eyes. Although many people go through similar processes at various times in their own life, they do so unconsciously, so they are not aware of the process or the magic unfolding and miracles happening. I'm not the only person who doesn't have a ladder holder. However, what I have come to understand is that manifestation does not require ladder holders, although it would be nice to have them. Instead it requires the willingness to hold a few ladders if necessary, but then to move to the level of Mastery.

Spiritual or metaphysical mastery, calls for the understanding and realization that there is no other person who is responsible for our growth and evolution. Because I'm on the path of spiritual and metaphysical mastery, I must not be looking for ladder holders. I must be willing to master the process of manifestation and no matter what teachers come my way along the path, I must be willing to maintain control of my efforts and my destiny.

The Awakening and Healing Retreat helped me to become more self-aware, and that is one of the greatest gifts that I could ask for in the process. As a doctor of Metaphysical Science, one of my callings is not to train leaders; but rather to create other Masters and then let us Masters share the room together to bring about an amazing paradigm shift in the world where all are empowered through the spirit of love.

My Message to You about
The Power of Metaphysical Science

I came to understand a long time ago that behind every physical reality is a spiritual one. What you see is not what you get because there are some things that our physical eyes may not see. There is a much greater power behind the carnal.

There is a biblical text that says, "For we wrestle not against flesh and blood, but against principalities, against powers, against the rulers of the darkness of this world, against spiritual wickedness in high places" (Eph. 6.12, KJV).

The message of this chapter is an encouragement to tap into a greater power that transcends the ugliness of this world. When the biblical text says we fight against principalities, powers, rulers of the darkness of this world, and against spiritual wickedness in high places, in essence it is saying that when we come with truth and light, our hostile encounters in this world are often not with the people, but rather with the lies, falsehood, ignorance, and spiritual blindness. Our battles are with the systems of belief that were founded on falsehood.

Any word that is not rooted in truth is a principle that light comes to dispel. Only light can dispel darkness and when we live in the light and operate in the principles of light, we can overcome the darkness of the world. There is nothing spooky about it. Metaphysical Science is an ancient science that reconciles the material with the spiritual and teaches a system of mastery that helps you to decisively activate your hidden power. The ideals that have been put forward in this world are not always based in truth. However, unless and until you change the core and measurement of what goes through you, will you be able to move the boundaries and limitations from which you operate. It is important to move the boundaries and limitations that govern your life, particularly when those boundaries hinder your progress and have been applied by an ungodly force to control you.

Chapter 9

Self-Awareness, Self-Worth, & Self-Value

"Measure the world inside out, not the other way around because what you see is what you put there. The good thing is, if you don't like it, you have the power to change it."

Self-awareness is fundamental to spiritual and meta-physical mastery. It took this retreat to help me become more conscious of who I am so that I could more readily master what I have. I'm not like other people. I'm not common therefore; I cannot allow myself to be handled in a common manner. Unfortunately, that is what I had done in the past. If I expect anyone to value me and see the inherent worth in me and my gifts, I must first demon-strate that value for myself and my gift.

During the retreat, I gave just about everything away. While I realize those were seeds that I was sowing for a future time, it is not necessary to give as much away as I did. Not only is it not necessary, it also is not helpful.

There were five people who helped to drive this message home loud and clear. They provided "food for thought." They were a classic example of why it is important to value yourself and your gifts. I learned a very important lesson through several people who participated or attended the Awakening and Healing Retreat. My behavior and how I handled myself in relation to other people is what opened the way for disrespect and lack of value.

I always told others that they had to teach people how to handle them. I was awakened to the fact that I really had a lot of teaching to do on my end, starting with myself. There was nothing else that needed to happen for me to get the Universe's message loud and clear. Although it is good to give, it is possible to give too much because when you give so much of yourself away, it does not allow people the opportunity to value you and what you have. I gave so much away in connection with this retreat and in my life that it prevented others from appreciating the inherent value and worth of me as a person and my gifts. I have been taken for granted in many of my relationships. I didn't like it, but until the Awakening and Healing Retreat, I had no idea why it was happening. It was a real awakening process.

I was giving way too much away, especially my time and energy. What sense does it make to give away so much and then struggle to pay the rent? That is plain foolishness. I was misreading situations and giving others the benefit of the doubt. I misread the mutuality of relationships. Because I felt one way about someone and valued them, did not mean they felt the same way. Someone's presence in your life or sphere does not always equal support. It is important to be able to discern the character and purpose of those who are in your sphere. Otherwise, you end up doing yourself and others a dis-service.

My Message to You about
Self-Awareness, Self-Worth, & Self-Value

I learned very early on that there was a greater power within and that I had the power to change many circumstances in my life. Yet, my trouble came not from the absence of that truth, but from the lack of self-confidence. External situations and experiences caused me to doubt my self-worth and question whether or not I was good enough or belonged in certain circles. I was bullied as a child and the impact of bullying can have that effect.

You have to teach people how to handle you. The best way to teach them is by handling yourself with love and respect. When you know who you are and know your worth, no matter whether or not someone else sees your value, you will inevitably demonstrate how you are to be treated.

You don't have to accept anything someone throws your way, regardless of your station in life. When you live according to the character of person you are and allow your carriage to be a demonstration of what you stand for, others will have no other option than to behave in a like manner where you are concerned. This does not mean that you will not interface with people who may try to push or test the boundaries; but the minute you stand on what you say you believe and stand on your truth with dignity and self-respect, others will know that it is a no-go when it comes to disrespecting you.

Be who you believe inside to be, regardless of where others try to box you in or position you. The only limitations you have in your life are the ones you place on yourself. So in other words, no matter who your parents are, no matter if you grew up in a trailer park or home or even in a segregated area some referred to as the "ghetto," that does not make YOU ghetto. Ignorant is the person who refers to another human being as ghetto.

Some people might even try to make you feel bad about yourself when you call them on their foolishness on how they behaved with respect to you, don't be disillusioned by someone else's ignorance. Stand on your truth and keep it moving. Stop letting people devalue you; but in order to do so, you must first start valuing yourself.

Chapter 10

Making Changes

"Look at change as simply a life-shower to wash away the staleness of life. Every now and again we need to have one to feel and look refreshed."

C hanges are always taking place. However, in considering the statement, "You need strong ladder holders," it forced me to ask myself the question, "Who are my ladder holders?" That question led me to examine the people in my circle without wishful thinking or rose-colored glasses. It forced me to be more truthful with myself than I have ever been. I asked myself an even harder question about who was around me. "Do I really choose the people who are around me and are they for my greater good?"

When I examined my sphere, I came to realize that the majority of those floating around were not the character of people I wanted or needed around me. It doesn't mean they are bad people, they are just not an energetic match for me. My mind went to the writers support group. The one who asked me to do the group could not find the time to do what he dreamed of doing. This is not an energetic match for me. After the retreat and after I took the week to myself to digest the past two months, I had made the decision to remove myself as facilitator of the group. The energy was no longer a match. Interestingly, I did not have to do that because Rob text me and asked me to meet with him. When I did, he said he wanted to put a pause on the writers support group because he just does not have time to give it his full attention. I was grateful. He thought I would be disappointed, I told him if he had not put a pause on it I would have been removing myself because in order for me to give my time and energy to this process, he must also make it a priority. I will not give quality time to casual situations. If I make the commitment to take on something, I give it my best. With respect to the writer's group, I kept the door open for one-offs should he choose to do so. What I learned is that some people are just not ready. I'm ready and what I have to offer requires that people are ready for it. Therefore, I must move on to spaces where people are ready to embark upon the journey of where my offering takes them. The same with the book club, I knew that she was not ready, and consequently, I just could not give the energy to organizing everything. When I stopped into the Artisan Café to push the start of the book club back a month, I learned the Jean had gone and got a full-time job and her daughter was running the café. When I went in she said to me that her mother was not ready to do the book club, so she has to put it on hold. I had already sensed that. Again, I was grateful.

During and after the Awakening and Healing Retreat, I had set my mind on change and was very specific in some of the areas that required change. It is interesting how once I accepted change, the Universe helped open the doors for change to happen with very little effort on my part. Some of those areas were not easy to swallow.

Looking at the areas where change was needed was very challenging for me because mainly it required me to look in the mirror. It required me to look at what I really wanted. I looked at me, I looked at my situation, I looked at my environment, my community, my family situation, my friendships, my professional relationships. I looked at everything I could think to look at. When I actually opened my eyes to who was in fact around me consistently, there was really no one there, and the one person who was there did not want to be there and he had already started making changes in his life to spend less and less time away. Time will tell the impact. While the time away from each other might have been a good thing, there is much anxiety in change and I wanted change, but I did not want it to happen all at one time. I did that before years ago and let me tell you, it is not easy.

When I looked at my inner circle, it was and is virtually empty. Those closest to me are my husband, my sister, children, and the memories of my mother. I realized I still had a lot of healing to do with respect to my mother. So in that situation, I have embarked upon a healing journey where grief is concerned. Yet even then, I had to assess my situation truthfully. None of my family members are what I would call ladder holders. They are as supportive as they can be. Ideally, what I would like to do is build a support system for them to have ease so that they can be effective helpers in my work. I would like to establish a platform where they can have a space to follow their dreams and live a life of purpose. I would like to offer them and others a space where they can become masters of their divine gifts for the greater good and retreat from the coldness and harshness of the world. I have in mind this utopian community where they can truly feel and be safe, feel and be loved, feel and be happy, feel and be healthy, feel and be at peace. A space where there is compassion and kindness.

I want to help change the way people approach life, help to create more positive emotions, help place people on the pathway to growth and evolution, increase in others a sense of purpose, expand and increase my resources that makes for a more meaningful and successful life, create a sense of oneness and universal flow, help myself and others experience more satisfaction in life.

When I think of the type of environment I want to create, I reflect back to the environment that Dr. Carl C. Bell gave me the opportunity to create in downstate Illinois. It was a space where you come to work, but there was freedom and your children and family were welcomed. As long as you got the work done, there was creative freedom. I was able to flow my best when not having someone look over my shoulders. That is the sort of environment I would like to create for my family and those who choose to come to work with me—a family, a community, a loving and peaceful environment where people can be free to be themselves, yet contribute to the overall success of the space. I know what it looks like, but more importantly, I know what it feels like. So I have been going about for years toward that goal. Yet, the Awakening and Healing Retreat helped me to see what changes were needed to be able to realize that dream in this lifetime.

I did not have anyone in my sphere who believed in me to say, I will hold the ladder for you to climb up as high as you can go. My mother was that for me, but she passed away in 2005. I've held many ladders in my time, but when it came down to having a ladder holder for me, they have been non-existent. My circumstances required me to reassess areas of my life and how I was doing things.

In the past, I've sought out mentors; I've sought out those who would help me figure things out. I've sought out those who could show me how to get to where I wanted to go and climb to the top. At the end of the day, I was unable to find or identify such a person as they were busy building their empire. I know there is a return on my investments and I have made plenty of them. I invested in others, and one day those returns are going to start coming in even though at that moment I was unable to find anyone to invest in me the way I was investing in others. I had to confront myself and have a heart-to-heart talk with Atiya. My truth shouted back to me like a thousand echoes.

"I must be willing to invest in myself!"

I must be willing to put myself first and give generously to myself in the same way if not more than I have given to others. I have to be willing to be my own advocate and champion my own cause. I must be willing to live unapologetically, speaking my truth, and stop allowing others to devalue me by first stopping the devaluing of self. I must believe in myself. I must first love myself.

As I looked into the mirror, the person looking back at me said very firmly, "It is time to change my sphere."

She removed the rose-colored glasses from my eyes. What I saw was not pleasing at all. She continued to speak to me. "There is no way that I am willing to continue in this paradigm."

She looked me square in the eyes. She was fierce. Yet, as I looked deeper into her eyes, a sense of power came over me. What was once fear, turned into amazing valor.

I looked at me again, and asked the questions.

- Who is in my inner sphere?

- Who is contributing to my life and work?

- What is the nature of the energy of those in my sphere?

- Do the people who are around me lift me up, leave me feeling energized, and good about myself? Or

- Do the people who are around me bring negative energy, leave me feeling ashamed of who and what I am, and/or energetically depleted?

- Am I able to be my authentic self around those in my sphere and am I able to speak my truth without having to feel like I have to hide my true feelings?

- Do those in my sphere value me, my feelings, and my work?

- Do the people in my sphere help to build my confidence or do they contribute to lowering my self-esteem and confidence?

My Message to You about
Making Changes

Change is a natural and necessary part of life. There have been times in my life where I welcomed it; other times I experienced anxiety at the very thought of it. Yet, no matter how much we may want things to stay the same, seasons change and learning to embrace the beauty of the changing seasons helps us to positively live a more empowered life in all seasons of our lives.

While seasons change, some changes in your life are well within your control, and it is these changes that I want to briefly speak about here. If you are in a space right now where you feel things have gone a bit stale and you could use a little freshness, whether that is in perspective, environment, associates, or something else fresh, try examining your sphere, shaking it up a bit, and seeing what gives. It could be that you indeed could use some revisions.

Change does not have to be something you dread, it can be fun, especially if you soberly become an active part of the process. When you set out to modify your life, it requires that you look in the mirror Don't be afraid of what you see, just envision a better picture and then go to work to take the necessary steps to create the sort of image you choose. Look at your life changes as your chance to get something new and better that more appropriately fits where you are right now.

Sometimes all it takes is a small shift and that little trans-formation can make a world of difference. The key to any change is to ensure that you are still being true to yourself and staying authentic. Also, don't change for anyone else, but you. When you make the changes in your life for your benefit, it sticks and everyone has gets the residual benefit from your growth.

Envision the changes you seek in your life, and then go about making them. Every change in you for the better is a positive change in the world. Imagine if everyone you know started making changes within themselves for the better, how much better place the world could be for all of us. You got this! Together, we got this!

Chapter 11

Making Choices

"Recognize the best in yourself and then choose to be that."

The above questions alone inspired me to delete people from my social media pages. Other questions forced me to confront the necessity to block others from having access to me online or offline.

From where I stand, there are five types of people who tend to take up space in your sphere outside of specific family members who support you the best they can.

The Five Types of People

1. Those who believe in you and demonstrate it by getting in the race with you, running all the way making sure to hold you up.

2. Those who come into your life for a season and a reason to impart what they were universally called to impart, and receive what they were universally supposed to receive and then continue on their life's journey. Often you don't see them again after their season in your life.

3. Those who cheer you on, offer encouraging words from the side-lines, but offer no real tangible support when it counts. Their word usually fails them or they remain quiet when you really need to hear from them.

4. Those who watch you struggle and will not even offer as much as a glass of water.

5. Those who linger in your midst, watch you struggle, secretly hoping you fail, and every chance they get, throw a stumbling block in your way.

When I looked at my situation, types three through five seemed to be taking up the majority of the space; and type two has been a running theme. Because of my soul mission, I understand why that was a running theme. However, the other types of people taking up space were not something I was willing to accept. It just was not, nor the energy I choose to be around. I have awakened to the danger of having those types of people in my space.

I take the responsibility for it though because I had allowed those relationships into my life. As such, now I'm doing the necessary letting go. I won't put on a facade. It is very challenging. This has been a difficult letting go because some of the people I have detached from are people that I really wanted to like me and find value in me in word and deed, not just lip service. I felt them to be important, I respected them, and I valued them. However, in my interactions with them, there was always this sense that I was not good enough or did not measure up. Also, there was this sense of feeling like they were somehow looking down on me or not valuing and respecting me in the same manner. No matter how often I tried to suppress the feelings I was having, they would constantly creep up and I would start feeling less than. That was not their issue that was mine. I did not fit in their sphere. My authentic values, beliefs, and true feelings were in contrary to what they would discuss, and I was always afraid to speak up for fear of losing the friendship or connection. Perhaps they felt it too. Sometimes when they would say something that I honestly believed to be so ridiculous, my response would be "that's interesting," or "wow." In some cases, I would just chuckle. I did not want to make waves. I wanted them to like me and see the beauty in me. The truth is I had to see the beauty in myself.

It was imperative to make some choices. I chose me. I chose to be my authentic self no matter what someone else has to say about it. There is no station in life a person holds that is above my station. Therefore, if my authenticity makes them feel uncomfortable or in any way inferior or superior to me, that is a problem they have to sort out. At the same time, in choosing me, I have to do right by me. Doing right by me is speaking my authentic truth and having the courage to be real no matter who is in my presence.

In saying it like it is, there are some people who are just too exhausting to be around. They require more energy than I have to give them. They are too critical, judgmental, or have too many expectations. I chose not to be in the presence of those people. They make it too difficult for me to be myself. If I feel like I cannot be myself around a person, I'm really not interested in being in their company. I chose to accept myself. If a person cannot accept me for who I am, then they do not deserve to be in my presence. I chose the freedom to be myself and being myself is not defined by the expectations of others, nor what others feel I should be. If you cannot deal with that then "Houston, I think we have a problem!" You just are not the right person for my sphere. We are energetically not a match.

The Right People for My Sphere

1. People who value themselves so they can in turn see the inherent value in me.

2. People who can see beyond what their physical eyes are confronted with and who believes in me and my vision.

3. People who are not blinded by their ego or motivated by money and who are willing to see the project through from beginning to end – sink or swim. People who are loyal.

4. People who are not stuck in religious dogma, labelling, hierarchy, and "isms."

5. People who are willing to use their gifts and operate within their calling unapologetically. People who are a Soul Match.

My Message to You about Making Choices

With every situation I have faced in life, one thing I realized which remained true for me is this: I had the choice of how I responded. I learned early on, as a matter of fact, it was a part of my upbringing, when I can recognize the best in myself, I can undoubtedly choose to be that regardless of what was going on outside of myself.

You cannot control how people behave or what they say, but what you can control is how you respond to it. Some things just don't even warrant an acknowledgement. If you have a vision for yourself and your life and that vision is rooted in alignment with what the Creator's vision for your life is, success is inevitable.

This might be an old cliché, but it remains true. If you can see it, you can be it. Regardless of what others try to make you or condition you to be, the key is being who you envision yourself to be regardless.

You are not what other say you are or call you, you are what you believe yourself to be internally, and that can go either way. Think positive thoughts of yourself and keep that ever present in the forefront of your consciousness and become the greater part of who you are. You are not your circumstances or your past mistakes. Once you start believing better of yourself that is the day you start living a better you.

Chapter 12

Reclaiming My ME!

"Bring back yourself into useful condition fit for cultivation. Till the soil of your greatness, plant the seeds of your divinity, and harvest the blessings of your being—product of the Most High."

The Awakening and Healing Retreat was a vehicle that took me to a place to recover, rescue, restore, redeem, recondition, and remodel ME! It was a personal journey, and truly a Soul Evolution Experience. As I recount my experience, it's like this.

An Awakening Moment is that moment you finally get the "aha" and wake up to the fact that there is a need and urgency to make some very real changes in your life and circumstances. For me, it was when I woke up to the fact that there was a need and urgency to re-assess my life and my relationships, but not from the other person's eye or perspective, rather from my own perspective and the truth of what I wanted and what is important for me.

Moving in Mid-Air is a reminder of what you must do when there is no support system or people around you willing to hold you up. You keep going! My reminder started as a feeling of being left hanging without help or the type of support I felt I needed to pull the retreat off. The way things unfolded and the way I was forced to move drove home the point that I have a supernatural power within and although things may not be the way I wanted them to be, it was important to keep going even without people around to support me and without a system of support. "I can do all things through…"

Pushing Past Fear, Doubt, and Disappointment is about overcoming stumbling blocks, obstacles, and potentially show-stopping issues. Your ego may present all sorts of mental challenges to confront, but that is when you have to thank your ego and politely tell it to go somewhere and sit down. The way the retreat came about and the process of planning it until its eventual manifestation was a lesson for me on how to move past disappointment to forgiveness and acceptance. People are not necessarily where I am in life and even those closest to me may not understand my vision. However, the message I received was that it is important to follow the path of my own destiny even if that means sometimes going it alone.

Choosing a Supportive Community is about learning how to keenly choose people to become a part of your circle. It is a science and one where if you plan on climbing to the top of the ladder in your life, you must choose objectively and not through the eyes of wishful thinking, emotion, or behind rose-colored glasses. At the retreat, I went through a reconditioning process and was admonished about casting my pearls before swine, sowing seeds on barren land, and sharing my gifts in an environment that lacked the appreciation, gratitude, and value of both me and my gifts. The retreat taught me how to better select people to engage with and to put even more thought into selecting places and environments to live and work. It stressed for me the necessity to thoroughly assess prior to investing time and energy into someone, someplace, or something. It also challenged me to stop accepting things that don't serve me well and to be willing to let things go no matter how valuable they are to me. I must ask the questions: Is there shared value? Is it a mutually beneficial relationship or situation or am I getting the shorter end of the stick?

A Life-Changing Lesson is the pointed lesson you learn along the way that becomes pivotal in your journey. The most valuable lesson that I learned at the Awakening and

Healing Retreat was about self-worth and to stop abusing, neglecting, and denying myself what I wanted and needed just to get others to come out and play. Being a hero to others and a zero to yourself does not make you a fan favorite. I had to urgently learn to stop the abuse and neglect of self and to give to myself first what I was so fervently giving to others.

Confronting My Truth is about actively stopping lying to yourself and denying the reality of a situation or your circumstances so that you can go ahead and deal with it effectively. For me it was about asking myself the tough questions and taking off the rose-colored glasses in the relationship (business and otherwise) area of my life. It was about looking at the situation the way it actually was rather than how I wanted it to be so that I can make the necessary adjustments that serves me well and for my higher good.

Learning to Let Go & Trust is the process of overcoming fear, trusting that the Universe is working on your behalf, and to stop worrying because everything works out precisely how it is supposed to work out for your highest good. It is about learning how to flow and not trying to control every little detail. During this retreat, things came full circle. Letting go and trusting for me was about letting go of the fear of what people would think of the real me and trusting that I am beautiful, I am worthy, I am wonderfully special and unique and the Universe is always working for my highest good. So it is okay to let go of the facades and just trust in the process. In letting go and trusting, all I have to do is authentically show up being fabulously me and move in my own uniqueness and Soul Mission.

The Power of Metaphysical Science is about learning how to master yourself and your circumstances instead of getting stuck on the ground because you don't have the physical comforts you desire. My experience taught me that I am what I am and I have what I have and that is way more powerful than what I can comprehend with my physical faculties. I realized that it is okay to give myself permission to use what I have to my greatest benefit and advantage.

Self-Awareness, Self-Worth, & Self-Value is about understanding who you are, what you are worth, and how valuable you are and actively demonstrating that in your everyday life. During the retreat for me this was a big one. I had to come to an understanding that for me, it's not about someone else's feelings when they overstep their boundaries where I'm concerned. It was about me speaking my truth and telling it like it is regardless of what others felt or thought. It was about not getting enmeshed in other people's ways and values, especially when they were out of alignment with my own. It was also about me identifying karmic interactions and opportunities for me to follow the North

Star in my life rather than respond to the whispers of the South or past.

Making Changes is that activity that forces you to complete a self-examination and analysis in order to sort out the problems in your life by first sorting out yourself. When you take the responsibility for everything in your life, you empower yourself to discover the solutions and make the necessary changes to you and your story. As I personally embarked upon that process, the necessary changes for me were in how I conducted myself with me, not other people. They were merely reflecting back to me how I was treating myself; and since I did not like the reflection I was seeing, I decided and went to work to make changes in me. Ultimately that changed my sphere.

Making Choices is about how you go about making conscious and intentional changes in your life. With change, it's personal; you examine yourself. With choices you examine your situation, your environment, and the people around you. The retreat helped me to courageously move to make better choices for myself and my life. I started making firmer decisions about who I would permit in my sphere and who I would give my energy to. I removed the "obligation" factor. I was reminded that I have choices and I chose to actively exercise my power of choice.

Reclaiming my ME! is check mate! When it comes to me, myself, and me loving self, there are no more trump cards that can be played. There are no more moves people can make to have me deny myself. I ex-communicated some folks and changed the game. Now it is about me defining me. It's about me achieving my ultimate potential and it's about me becoming the best part of myself and making my rare and unique qualities some of the greatest contributions the world has ever known. I'm reclaiming my ME. I'm not settling, and I'm no longer denying myself the life that God has promised me. I invite you to do the same!

I bow and take my hat off to ME! And . . . I'm doing it with a SMILE. "Booyah!"

Other Works by Dr. Atiya

OTHER BOOKS BY DR ATIYA

- From Ordinary to Extraordinary – 978-0-9916444-0-7 (multiple formats available)

- Petals of a Rose – 978-0-9916444-4-5 (multiple formats available)

- Purposeful Dating – 978-0-9916444-1-4 (multiple formats available)

- The Beauty of Being Free – 978-0-9916444-2-1 (multiple formats available)

- Overcoming the Pain of Losing a Mother (multiple formats available)

- Love is Not a Game (multiple formats available)

- Hidden Pearls (eBook)

- Safari With Soul: ABC's in the Wild – 978-0-9968672-3-8 (Children's Book Series)

- The Adventures of Master Junior Jones: The Birth of a Super Adventurer – 978-0-9968672-2-1 (Children's Book)

- The Lesson of the Butterfly (multiple formats available only on website)
- We Shall Come Forth (multiple formats available only on website)

AUDIO MESSAGES AVAILABLE ON THE WEBSITE

- Get Fit, Fabulous, and Develop the Heart of a Champion
- This is Atiya
- Balancing Family, Friends, and Frenemies
- The Circle of Life: Breaking the Cycles and Bonds of Generational Curses
- Keeping Your Eyes on the Prize
- Why Black Men Don't Marry Black Women
- Learning to Respect Your Spouse
- Building Trust in Your Relationship
- Move Your Relationship From Casual to Courtship
- SFT (StraightForward Talk) Collection

MEDITATION PROGRAMS

- 21-Day Twin Soul Journey of the Heart

<u>SIGNATURE OFFERINGS</u>

- Soul Fidelity for Individuals
- Soul Fidelity for Companies

Bibliographic Index

"BibleGateway." 1John 4:4 KJV - - Bible Gateway, www.biblegateway.com/passage/?search=1John%2B4%3A4 &version=KJV.

Chand, Samuel R. *Who's Holding Your Ladder.* Whitaker House, 2015.

Chand, Samuel R. "Who's Holding Your Ladder? ." Atlanta.

"Erykah Badu – Bag Lady." *Genius*, 21 Nov. 2000, genius.com/Erykah-badu-bag-lady-lyrics.

"Hebrews 11:1." The Holy Bible Illustrated, Printed at His Majesty's Printers, p. 834.

Schwartz, Stephen, and Hans Zimmer. "Stephen Schwartz (Ft. Michelle Pfeiffer & Sally Dworsky) – When You Believe." Genius, 17 Nov. 1998, genius.com/Stephen-schwartz-when-you-believe-lyrics.

About the Author

Dr. Atiya K Jones

A dynamic and charismatic transformational genius and visionary with HEART, Dr. Jones specializes in Soul Evolution and whole life transformation. She is a metaphysician, author, and seasoned spiritual guide with exceptional intuitive & psychic gifts who has an uncanny ability to help people release unlimited power and potential; call forth their creative spirit and passion; increase their creative energy; and experience profound manifestation.

A teacher of meditation and Kundalini Yoga, Reiki Master, and the creator of Soul Fidelity, Dr. Jones' work also involve transforming lives & communities; unearthing potential & possibility; and driving individual & organizational success through soul mission work. Dr. Jones is the author of several books, including *From Ordinary to Extraordinary*; *The Beauty of Being Free*; and *Purposeful Dating*, as well as the producer of several empowerment messages, a number of self-help articles, essays and writings dealing with spirituality, health and wellness, marriage and relationships, cultural competence, and self-empowerment.

She is known as Mrs. Illinois International 2004 and third runner-up worldwide; for lecturing at colleges and universities, ministering in various spiritual houses, and speaking at numerous events throughout America, Europe, the Caribbean, and Canada. Also, Dr. Jones appears in several newspaper articles and magazines, and on numerous radio and television programs throughout the world.

Dr. Jones is the recipient of countless awards in the performing arts, community service, and other areas including a Going the Extra Mile Monetary Award from Dr. Carl C. Bell and the Community Mental Health Council, Inc. (CMHC) for her work in Child Welfare Reform.

www.ingramcontent.com/pod-product-compliance
Lightning Source LLC
Chambersburg PA
CBHW060904280326
41934CB00007B/1180